PRACTICAL GUIDES

GOVERNMENT GRANTS

A Guide for Voluntary Organisations

Maggie Jones was born in London in 1953 and read biological sciences at Exeter University.

She has worked for a number of voluntary organisations including the Family Planning Association, where she edited *Family Planning Today*; the International Planned Parenthood Federation, as a staff writer on their quarterly development magazine, *People*, and as editor of *IPPF News*; and the National Council for Voluntary Organisations, where she was editor of the Practical Guides series.

She is now a freelance writer and author of several books, including *Voluntary Organisations and the Media* (Bedford Square Press, 1984), *Trying to Have a Baby* (Sheldon Press, 1984), *Everything You Need to Know about Adoption* (Sheldon Press, 1987) and *Safety and Your Child* (Conran Octopus, 1989). She has contributed to a variety of newspapers and magazines, including the *Observer*, the *Independent*, the *Guardian* and *Parents'* magazine on health, childcare and other women's issues.

Government Grants
A Guide for Voluntary Organisations

Compiled by Maggie Jones

*Illustrations
by
Christine Roche*

Bedford Square Press

Published by
BEDFORD SQUARE PRESS of the
National Council for Voluntary Organisations
26 Bedford Square, London WC1B 3HU

© NCVO 1980, 1983, 1986, 1988, 1989

All rights reserved. No part of this publication may be reproduced or transmitted, in any form or by any means, electronic, mechanical, photocopying, recording or otherwise, without the prior permission of the publisher.

First published 1980 as *Sources of Statutory Money: A guide for voluntary organisations*
Second edition 1983
Reprinted with corrections 1984
Third edition 1986
Fourth edition 1988
Fifth edition 1989

Typset by BookEns, Saffron Walden, Essex

Printed and bound in England by
J. W. Arrowsmith Ltd, Bristol

British Library Cataloguing in Publication Data

Government grants: a guide for voluntary
organisations. – 5th ed.
– (Practical guides)
1. Great Britain. Voluntary organisations.
Grants. Sources: Government agencies –
Directories
I. Jones, Maggie, *1953*–   II. Series
361.7

ISBN 0-7199-1247-4

Contents

Introduction	1
How to use the guide	4

1 Grants from Central Government Departments

Defence	8
Education and Science	8
Energy	11
Environment	12
Foreign and Commonwealth Office	20
Health	20
Home Office	24
Lord Chancellor's Department	27
Overseas Development Administration	27
Trade and Industry	30
Transport	30

2 Grants from Organisations* Authorised to Allocate Government Money

Arts Council of Great Britain	32
British Film Institute	33
British Library	34
Commission for Racial Equality	34
Countryside Commission for England and Wales	36

*non-governmental bodies as defined in the Civil Service Department 1978 Survey of Fringe Bodies

Crafts Council	37
Equal Opportunities Commission	38
Health Education Authority	39
Housing Corporation	40
Nature Conservancy Council	41
Regional Arts Associations	43
Rural Development Commission	44
Sports Council	46
Tourist Boards	48
Training Agency	50
Youth Exchange Centre	57

3 Money from Europe

European Social Fund	58
Other Sources of EEC Money	58

4 Grants from Local Authorities

Background	61
Legal Framework of Local Government	63

Appendices

1 How to Apply for a Grant	69
2 Relations between the Voluntary Sector and Government: A Code for Voluntary Organisations	73
3 Powers under which Local Authorities Can Fund Voluntary Organisations	75
List of Further Reading	80
Index	81

INTRODUCTION

The fifth edition of *Government Grants: A Guide for Voluntary Organisations* comes at a particularly significant period in the provision of public sector funding for voluntary organisations. Total public sector support for voluntary organisations in 1986/87 was estimated by the Charities Aid Foundation to be £4,147 million, including tax concessions. Yet within this seemingly large figure important changes are beginning to take place.

First we must remember that the two largest components of this sum are government grants to housing associations and societies (£1,048 million), and what was then the Manpower Services Commission (£660 million). The former are set to increase dramatically as a result of government policy and legislation; indeed, it is estimated that within two or three years housing associations will be building more new houses than local authorities. However, linked to this dramatic increase is a concern that housing associations' important role in meeting special needs will be lost through an emphasis on mainstream provision and a need to charge higher rents.

The Manpower Services Commission has now been abolished and the Community Programme, which provided £480 million funding to voluntary organisations in 1986/87, has been replaced by the Employment Training (ET) Scheme. These changes are having a dramatic effect on the voluntary sector, particularly on local community and rural projects. Although overall levels of funding to the voluntary sector may remain much the same under ET, a large number of projects providing social services and undertaking environmental and building work are having to close or reduce their activities, since their operations do not easily satisfy the new requirements.

Many of these projects are now looking to their local authorities for support, yet they are in no position to help. Local authority funding of the voluntary sector has fallen for the second year running to £402 million in 1986/87. One of the main reasons for this was the abolition of the GLC and metropolitan counties, which saw a shift towards central government funding of local groups as a result of the various post-abolition arrangements. However, most of these arrangements are on a tapering basis, so that gradually the burden on local government will increase. Add to this the effects of time expiry in the Urban Programme, and the impact of ratecapping and grant penalties, which has begun to have severe effects on the voluntary sector in some areas such as Brent and Camden, and the prospects for obtaining new funding from local authorities are bleak indeed.

What is perhaps more promising as a source of funding over the coming years is a shift towards payment for services, as opposed to arm's length grant aid. There is now general acceptance that we are moving towards more pluralistic models of service provision, both as a result of competitive tendering and as a result of policy changes resulting from reviews such as the Griffiths report on community care. Voluntary organisations will need to think their way through these new developments extremely carefully – to ensure their own role is not distorted, to secure their own survival and, most important of all, to ensure the consumer is provided with the best possible service.

There is evidence of a similar type of shift taking place within central government funding. Central government departments gave £279.5 million in 1986/87. This represents an overall increase of just 1.1 per cent in real terms since 1985/86. The terms and conditions of this funding are increasingly reflecting government policies and priorities. For example, the Urban Programme, whose support for the voluntary sector is now declining, has put increasing emphasis on economic and environmental projects at the expense of social projects. Other government departments are requiring clearer evidence of how voluntary organisations' activities relate to their own policy objectives and are asking for detailed information on performance indicators to demonstrate efficiency and effectiveness. Some departments are undertaking reviews of their grant programmes within this type of framework.

At one level this is no more than good practice. Any funder will be looking for some correspondence between their policy objectives and the work of the voluntary organisations they fund. Likewise any funder has the right to expect efficiency, effectiveness and accountability from those they fund. There is, however, a balance to be struck between these requirements and the equally important requirements of independence and self-determination. After all, it is these characteristics which lie at the heart of the voluntary sector and which differentiate it from the public sector. We must be careful to get the balance right.

There are also some other issues surrounding central government funding of increasing concern to many national organisations. One is the vexed question of cash limits. Annual increases of 2½ per cent represent an effective cut, and after a number of years under this regime many organisations are feeling the pinch.

Another issue is the growing tendency to require private sector funding to match public sector support. Most voluntary organisations recognise the need to try and involve the private sector in their work, but many have found it extremely difficult to obtain anything other than small pieces of one-off funding from this source. This experience is confirmed by the Charity Aid Foundation's statistics for 1986/87, which show that the 400 largest giving companies only give 0.2 per cent of their profits to voluntary organisations, whilst the average size of a donation from small companies is only £200. Furthermore, voluntary organisations' appeal to the private sector varies enormously: 'unpopular' causes such as the mentally ill, victims of AIDS and disadvantaged minorities usually have little prospect of raising money from companies.

One other, more optimistic, development is that health authorities, which are directly funded by central government, are increasing their support for the voluntary sector. Admittedly, funding was starting at a low base, but total grants from health authorities to voluntary organisations rose by 38 per cent to £25.2 million between 1985/86 and 1986/87.

Public sector funding of the voluntary sector is likely to become an increasingly contentious issue over the coming years. However, the requirements for those seeking grants remain the same – clear information about the different grant programmes available, with advice about how and when to apply. We hope that this fifth edition of *Government Grants* will continue to satisfy this requirement.

Usha Prashar
Director of the National Council for Voluntary Organisations

HOW TO USE THE GUIDE

The guide brings together information about grants from central government departments; from quangos; from local authorities; and from the European Commission. Its intention is to provide groups with guidance about whether they would be eligible for a particular source of grant aid.

Each entry gives general information about the types of grant given and the sort of work which can be funded. Wherever possible the guide includes examples of projects which have received funding. Contacts are given for further information. In most cases this is the name of the official dealing with a particular grants programme, but it needs to be remembered that these names may change during the life of this edition of the guide.

Criteria for grant aid may be reviewed at any time. Before applying for a grant it is therefore essential to talk to the department, organisation or local authority concerned.

Throughout the book, references to a single year, for example 1987/88, indicate a financial year unless stated otherwise.

The guide is primarily aimed at groups in England. Groups in other countries in the UK can get information from the following:

Wales
Wales Council for Voluntary Action
Llys Ifor
Crescent Road
Caerffili CF8 1XL
Tel: (0222) 869224/5/6

WCVA produces *the Wales Funding Handbook for Community Groups and Voluntary Organisations in Wales* (1988). WCVA can also provide information about grants in Wales.

Scotland
Scottish Council for Voluntary
   Organisations
18–19 Claremont Crescent
Edinburgh EH7 4HX
(031) 556 3882

SCVO and the Scottish Community Education Council have produced *Funds for Your Project: A Practical Guide for Community Groups and Voluntary Organisations in Scotland* (1988). The SCVO information department can help with enquiries about grants in Scotland.

Northern Ireland
Northern Ireland Council for
  Voluntary Action
127 Ormeau Road
Belfast BT7 1SH
(0232) 321224

NICVA can help with enquiries about grants in Northern Ireland or consult *The Funding Handbook: A Guide to Money Available for Community and Voluntary Initiatives in Ireland* (1988), available from Creative Activity for Everyone, 23–25 Moss Street, Dublin 2, tel. (0001) 770330.

Thanks are due to the many people who gave information which has been used in this guide.

CENTRAL GOVERNMENT GRANTS TO VOLUNTARY ORGANISATIONS 1980/81–1986/87[1]

Department	1980/81 £	1981/82 £	1982/83 £	1983/84 £	1985/86 £	1986/87 £
Agriculture, Fisheries and Food	69,500	92,900	90,900	99,400	117,700	171,700
Defence	2,004,000	2,637,000	2,361,000	2,634,990	3,543,815	4,825,762
Education and Science[2]	11,454,000	12,381,000	11,175,000	14,317,606	18,089,079	16,229,814
Employment[3]	21,391,000	23,207,000	26,380,000	27,720,000	30,316,000	33,294,000
Energy[4]		91,000	134,000	91,000	865,000	1,118,000
Environment						
– direct grants[5]	682,914	762,560	975,666	1,219,888	2,566,366	3,612,417
– urban programme[6]	22,000,000	27,000,000	37,500,000	46,500,000	76,300,000	76,011,000
Foreign and Commonwealth Office[7]	523,694	584,411	9,030,548	11,519,597	32,255,657	880,626
Health and Social Security[8]	12,247,052	13,775,245	15,462,000	23,122,709	32,045,917	35,075,544
Home Office	14,466,315	15,396,295	15,558,717	16,890,250	18,300,275	19,541,336
Industry	500,856	479,000	660,000	(see Trade)		
Lord Chancellor's Department	469,302	528,673	583,000	604,160	691,476	726,743
Northern Ireland Office[9]	16,884,666	20,397,823	9,480,597	12,091,327	16,801,124	14,974,781
Overseas Development Administration[10]	5,709,000	6,393,486	—	—	—	26,822,713
Scottish Office[11]						
– direct grants	4,740,515	5,515,032	6,499,630	6,823,494	8,247,195	8,970,443
– urban programme	1,007,000	3,188,877	4,897,000	6,750,000	11,700,000	16,600,000
Trade[12]	4,063,000	4,965,000	5,600,322	6,221,000	8,063,455	8,689,088
Transport	423,217	451,000	440,000	509,000	605,000	636,000
Welsh Office						
– direct grants	1,929,053	2,477,789	3,280,396	3,821,203	5,093,652	8,467,801
– urban programme[13]	243,562	690,000	861,613	1,325,000	2,375,000	2,850,000
	120,808,646	140,983,541	150,970,389	182,269,624	267,976,711	279,497,768

	1982/83 £	1983/84 £	1985/86 £	1986/87 £
Manpower Services Commission TOTAL	138,810,000	285,300,000	506,230,000	—
Community Enterprise Programme*	50,650,000	—	—	—
Youth Opportunities Programme†	86,700,000	81,000,000	132,400,000	125,000,000
Voluntary Projects Programme	980,000	4,300,000	7,830,000	8,250,000
Community Programme	480,000	200,000,000	366,000,000	480,000,000

*The Community Enterprise Programme was replaced in 1983 by the Community Programme.
†The Youth Opportunities Programme was replaced in 1983/84 by the Youth Training Scheme.

Notes to Table

1. Incorporates figures supplied by the Voluntary Services Unit, Home Office.
2. The 1979/80 figure included grants made to certain adult education bodies (mostly the extra-mural departments of universities). These have been omitted in subsequent years because they are no longer considered to fall into the category of voluntary organisations. The reduction between 1981/82 and 1982/83 results from the transfer to local government of responsibility for grant aiding local voluntary capital projects for the youth service and for village halls and community centres.
3. These monies are administered through the Manpower Services Commission and relate to sheltered employment and Community Industry schemes (see main guide). The 1982/83 and 1983/84 figures do not include MSC payments, given above.
4. Figures relate to a new energy conservation programme introduced in 1981/82 (see main guide).
5. Includes contributions from Department of Education and Science, Department of Health and Social Security and Department of Transport.
6. England only (see also Scottish Office and Welsh Office).
7. The 1982/83 and 1983/84 figures are combined figures, including Overseas Development Administration given separately in previous years. The 1983/84 figure includes the ODA total of £10,771,960, to British voluntary organisations only.
8. Includes £2,600,000 to support Opportunities for Volunteering, a new programme introduced in 1982/83.
9. In 1982/83 and 1983/84, figures have been re-calculated to exclude support under the Manpower Services Commission programmes for the unemployed (included in 1981/82 figure) and to housing associations (included in 1979/80 and 1980/81 figures). Comparative figures for other years would have been 1979/80: £3,820,879; 1980/81: £4,352,201; 1981/82: £5,667,904.
10. During 1986/87 there was a decrease in requests from voluntary agencies for grants in support of disaster, refugee and other emergency relief measures. That programme is, by its nature, reactive rather than planned. The other forms of support from the aid programme for voluntary agencies for their longer term development work increased substantially during 1986/87.
11. The 1983/84 figures for direct grants and urban programme are estimates. The 1982/83 figure for the urban programme is also an estimate.
12. Listed separately under Industry and Trade in previous years.
13. Includes £230,000 for Opportunities for Volunteering.

1
Grants from Central Government Departments

MINISTRY OF DEFENCE

The Ministry of Defence provides grants to some voluntary organisations for army welfare work and towards administrative or headquarters costs. Examples include SSAFA, the Red Cross, the Order of St John, Royal British Legion, Council of Voluntary Welfare Work, and Women's Royal Voluntary Service. However, there is no general fund to which voluntary bodies can apply.

Further information from:
Ministry of Defence
Empress State Building
Lillie Road
London SW6 1TR
(01) 385 1244

DEPARTMENT OF EDUCATION AND SCIENCE

There are three major types of grant aid to voluntary organisations from the DES:
- grants to voluntary youth organisations
- grants for adult education
- educational services and research funds

Grants to Voluntary Youth Organisations

There are four types of grant to youth organisations:
- headquarters grants
- capital grants
- innovatory grants

In 1985/86, DES grants to the Youth Service totalled nearly £4.5 million.

Headquarters grants
Nearly 70 national voluntary youth organisations are on a list of bodies eligible to bid for funding against a list of programme categories, which is reviewed annually. To be eligible, an organisation either has to have a headquarters plus branches or affiliated associations or it has to provide services to young people over a substantial area. There are also other more detailed criteria which an organisation has to meet, which are detailed in an annual grant memorandum. The applications for programme funding are considered by an HMI specialist adviser.

Capital grants
These are available to voluntary organisations for providing residential social and recreational facilities, on a national or regional basis, for young people aged between 14 and 20.

To be accepted as 'regional', the facility must attract users from a wide area of the country, covering at least four counties.

The grant will not exceed 50 per cent of the total agreed cost.

Innovatory grants
These are intended for innovative projects run by national voluntary youth organisations or by other organisations if the project is seen as relevant to the youth service as a whole. A priority is projects dealing with difficult or previously unexplored areas of work. The grants are for a maximum of three years, but shorter pilot schemes are welcome.

Adult Education Bodies

There are three types of grant given to adult education bodies:

- **Workers Educational Association Districts**
  The DES provides over half the costs of the 15 WEA districts running adult education courses in England.

- **Grants to relevant national associations**
  Organisations which receive funding include the National Institute of Adult Continuing Education, the Adult Literacy and Basic Skills Unit, and the National Union of Townswomen's Guilds. The grants are intended to help support the running of national bodies whose work stimulates locally provided adult education.

- **Long-term residential colleges**
  Six colleges are currently receiving grants.

Research and Certain Educational Services

Grants may be made to recognised organisations (other than local education authorities) towards:
- the development of educational methods either by way of educational research or the provision for that purpose of educational services
- other educational research
- the provision of educational services of an advisory or organising character

These grants are made through the Education Act 1944, S. 100(1)(b). In 1985/86 they totalled £14.8 million.

Organisations which receive grants from this source include the Pre-School Playgroups Association.

Further information from:
Department of Education and
Science
Elizabeth House
York Road
London SE1 7PH
(01) 934 9000

Enquiries about grants to voluntary youth organisations should be made to the Youth Service Unit. Enquiries about grants to adult education bodies should be made to Further and Higher Education Branch III. Educational services and research are dealt with by different branches, and separate enquiries should be made in each case.
  This information applies only to England.
  For information about Wales, contact the Welsh Office.
  For information about Scotland, contact the Scottish Education Department.
  For information about Northern Ireland, contact the Northern Ireland Office.

DEPARTMENT OF ENERGY

Draughtproofing, Insulation and Energy Advice Projects

There are three types of grants available to Training Managers who wish to run energy projects under Employment Training (ET) in England, Scotland and Wales.

Project preparation grants
Project preparation grants are intended to help ET Training Managers plan and promote local draughtproofing, insulation and energy advice projects. This maximum grant of £800 covers costs of postage, telephone, promotional meetings and a fee to undertake a feasibility study.

Project grants
These are grants to assist with the start-up costs of energy projects run by ET Training Managers. They are not available to meet running costs. Grants are partially recoverable at the end of the project and can cover:
- cost of purchasing necessary transport
- cost of purchasing other necessary equipment (tools, ladders, protective clothing)
- cost of producing an initial stock of publicity material to advertise project services

The basic maximum grant is £5,000, and there is a £9,000 maximum grant available for large projects or projects covering a large geographical area.

Project training grants
Project training grants assist with the cost of up to three days' training for new managers and supervisors of ET energy projects. This training includes visits to and by a well-established project, or attendance at approved training courses. The maximum grant is £300 and covers travel and subsistence costs, project fees and approved course fees.

These grant structures are currently under review and Training Managers are advised to contact Neighbourhood Energy Action (NEA) (or Energy Action Scotland for Scottish Training Managers) for further information.

Registration with NEA is a condition for eligibility, and Training Managers should discuss their proposals in advance with NEA or Energy Action Scotland.

Further information from:

Alan Hewitt
Neighbourhood Energy Action
2/4 Bigg Market
Newcastle upon Tyne
NE1 1UW
(091) 261 5677

Bill Craig
Energy Action Scotland
21 West Nile Street
Glasgow
G1 2PJ
(041) 226 3064

DEPARTMENT OF THE ENVIRONMENT

The Department of the Environment funds voluntary organisations through a range of programmes. The types of grant given are:
- Special Grants Programme
- Homelessness
- Urban Programme

The DoE publishes a guide to its grants to voluntary organisations. This can be obtained free of charge from:

Room P2/110
ICD2 Division
Department of the Environment
2 Marsham Street
London SW1P 3EB
(01) 276 4432

Special Grants Programme

From 1984/85, the DoE has operated a Special Grants Programme. There are two main types of grants:

Management grants
These are intended to help meet the administrative costs of mainly national voluntary bodies whose activities improve the efficiency and effectiveness of voluntary action in fields relevant to the DoE's interests.

Project grants
These are intended primarily to enable voluntary organisations to undertake innovatory or experimental projects of national significance relevant to DoE interests.

Voluntary organisations will need to be involved in one or more of the following activities:
- practical conservation or improvement work in the natural or man-made environment
- provision of education and information on aspects of the natural or man-made environment
- advisory services to members of the public or local groups on planning or other environmental subjects
- involving local residents in practical schemes for the regeneration of urban areas
- co-ordination, assistance or training of voluntary bodies engaged in one or more of these activities

Grants are normally limited to 50 per cent of revenue costs. They are generally awarded towards specified administrative activities and expenses, as agreed with the DoE, for up to three years, renewable annually. Each grant will be subject to regular monitoring arrangements and review.

The size of grant will vary according to the needs of the organisation but a typical grant will be between £5,000 and £40,000.

Applications are usually required by the end of October for grants commencing in April the following year.

In 1989/90, £2 million is expected to be available for the Special Grants Programme.

Further information from:
John Sherman
ICD2 Division
Room P2/110
2 Marsham Street
London SW1P 3EB
(01) 276 4455

Homelessness

Part III of the Housing Act 1985 places the responsibility for dealing with homelessness on local housing authorities.

Grants or loans can be given by the Department of the Environment to voluntary organisations concerned with homelessness or matters relating to homelessness, under S. 73 of the above Act.

Grants can be made towards the administrative costs of housing advice projects which are either national, regional or Londonwide in scope or innovative in nature. The provision, equipping or management of accommodation is not eligible for grant aid.

In the case of organisations funded so far, 'housing advice' has been taken to include advice designed to help solve the accommodation problems of people who are actually homeless or likely to become so. This has included advice on the homelessness legislation and other relevant legislation, such as that relating to security of tenure and protection from eviction. It has also encompassed advice about obtaining accommodation, e.g. in hostels, housing association or local authority property, and the private rented sector.

Grant recipients are normally expected to fund at least one-third and sometimes two-thirds of their expenditure from other sources, depending on the extent of their geographical coverage.

A request for the application form for a particular financial year can be made from November onwards in the preceding year, but it is advisable to make informal enquiries first.

In 1987/88, grant provision totalled £615,000 and individual grants ranged from £6,480 to £140,000.

Further information from:
J C Q Rowett
Room N8/10A
Department of the Environment
2 Marsham Street
London SW1P 3EB
(01) 276 3243

Urban Programme

The Urban Programme is the collective term for projects and activities supported by central government under the 1969 Local Government (Special Needs) Act and the 1978 Inner Urban Areas Act. These Acts give the DoE the power to pay grants to local authorities which have to spend money because of severe urban deprivation in their areas.

The Urban Programme is a mechanism for central government to enable local government to tackle economic, environmental and social problems through innovative projects. The projects may be run by local authority departments or voluntary organisations. Money is also made available to the private sector and to health authorities. Projects supported through the Urban Programme receive a grant from DoE to cover 75 per cent of their costs – the other 25 per cent must be paid out of the local authorities' own funds. DoE must approve all expenditure planned by local authorities under the Urban Programme.

The distribution of Urban Programme money depends on an annual round of negotiations between central government, local government and voluntary organisations. In 1987/88 some £77 million was channelled through the

Urban Programme to support innovative voluntary and community projects.

The programme funds four categories of projects: economic, environmental, social and housing. Economic schemes aim to encourage job creation – mini-factory units, for example, or access roads to industrial estates. Most voluntary economic schemes are concerned with training and advice-giving. Environmental schemes include housing and general environmental improvements and voluntary projects such as city farms. Housing schemes usually aim to improve estates. Until recently, most voluntary schemes have fallen into the 'social' category, which includes community centres, projects for old or handicapped people, the arts and children's play schemes. Although the present government has shifted the emphasis towards economic and environmental schemes, projects of all four kinds are still being supported in most areas. Projects run for or by black people have received increasing amounts of Urban Programme money, rising to £33 million by 1984/85.

In August 1986 the DoE announced changes in the Urban Programme. Resources are now targeted on just 57 districts and boroughs in England as listed below. Nine are described as *Partnership authorities* and the other 48 as *Programme authorities*. Together the 57 authorities are known as the Inner Area Programme or IAP authorities.

Inner City Partnerships (9)

Birmingham	Islington	Manchester
Gateshead	Lambeth	Newcastle
Hackney	Liverpool	Salford

(Manchester/Salford and Newcastle/Gateshead work together as single Partnerships).

Programme authorities (48)

Barnsley	Hammersmith	Lewisham	Sefton
Blackburn	& Fulham	Middlesbrough	Sheffield
Bolton	Haringey	Newham	South Tyneside
Bradford	Hartlepool	North Tyneside	Southwark
Brent	Hull	Nottingham	Stockton on Tees
Bristol	Kensington	Oldham	Sunderland
Burnley	& Chelsea	Plymouth	Tower Hamlets
Coventry	Kirklees	Preston	Walsall
Derby	Knowsley	Rochdale	Wandsworth
Doncaster	Langbaurgh	Rotherham	Wigan
Dudley	Leeds	St. Helens	Wirral
Greenwich	Leicester	Sandwell	Wolverhampton
Halton			The Wrekin

The 57 eligible authorities must each produce an IAP document identifying needs, policies and priorities for spending and which projects are put forward for funding. The IAP document is then submitted to DoE for approval. The nine Partnership authorities have an overall committee chaired by a government minister which considers and approves spending plans.

The community is supposed to be consulted and one of the benefits of the Inner Area Programme should be that voluntary groups have more say in how resources are used locally. Voluntary groups should find out how their authority consults the voluntary sector and make sure that they are involved. It can take a year from the time the voluntary organisation makes an initial approach to the authority to the receipt of any Urban Programme grant.

Derelict Land Grant

In England grants are available both to local authorities and others for the reclamation of derelict land for the purpose of bringing it into beneficial use or improving its appearance.

In Assisted Areas and Derelict Land Clearance Areas grants are at the rate of 100 per cent for local authorities and 80 per cent for others. Outside these areas the rate of grant is 50 per cent, except in national parks and areas of outstanding natural beauty where local authorities can receive 75 per cent.

In 1988/89, £77 million is available – £65.5 million for local authorities and £11.5 million for other applicants.

Urban Development Corporations

Urban Development Corporations (UDCs) are one of the main planks of the government's urban regeneration policy. The first UDCs, London Docklands Development Corporation and Merseyside Development Corporation, were set up in 1981. In 1987, UDCs were set up in the Black Country, Tyne & Wear, Teeside, Trafford Park and Cardiff Bay with mini-UDCs in Leeds and Bristol. A UDC in Sheffield was created in early 1988.

All the UDC areas have large tracts of derelict land and buildings; their boundaries have been drawn, in the main, to exclude existing populated areas.

The purpose of each UDC is to regenerate its designated area concentrating on the physical infrastructure – reclaiming land, rebuilding roads, providing new commercial premises. Public money is used to lever private sector investments and development into the area. Each UDC devises a local strategy for its area which also includes social, community and leisure provision.

At the time of writing, the newer UDCs were drawing up their strategies and few had *clear* policies for involving the voluntary sector, although most had set aside sums for a grant-aid programme for voluntary organisations. In London Docklands, there are grants programmes for capital, project and revenue support for community and voluntary groups working within the Urban Development Area. In Merseyside, Development Corporation grants have gone to voluntary organisations involved or connected to water recreation. The grants programmes will depend on the local priorities of each UDC.

To find out more you should contact the appropriate UDC office. The local council for voluntary service or other umbrella organisation should know about the local policies of their UDC.

For further information or advice about the Urban Programme or Urban Development Corporation contact:
Inner Cities Unit
NCVO
26 Bedford Square
London WC1B 3HU
(01) 636 4066

Urban Conservation and Historic Buildings

On 1 April 1984 responsibility for historic buildings grants passed from the Department of the Environment to the Historic Buildings and Monuments Commission for England. The Commission, or English Heritage, to give it its more familiar title, is responsible for three main types of grant aid for historic buildings. Voluntary bodies can be considered for all three of these grants.

Section 3A grants
Grants may be given to owners (including voluntary bodies) under S. 3A of the Historic Buildings and Ancient Monuments Act 1953, for the repair of buildings of outstanding historic or architectural interest, in national terms. The fact that a building has been statutorily listed under the Town and Country Planning Act 1971, as of *special* architectural or historic interest, does not necessarily mean that it is *outstanding*: each case is considered on its merits by English Heritage, with advice from its Historic Buildings Advisory Committee. The standard is very high – overall, only the top 2 to 3 per cent of buildings are likely to qualify.

Section 3A grant is usually given towards the cost of comprehensive major repairs to the historic structure of the building. Routine repairs and maintenance do not qualify for grant. It may also be offered for repairs to associated buildings, for example forming part of an outstanding garden, which are not outstanding in their own right, and for the conservation of objects, such as furniture, historically associated with an outstanding building or garden, though reserves for such objects are limited.

Section 10 grants
Grants may be given under S. 10 of the Town and Country Planning (Amendment) Act 1972, towards expenditure which will make a significant contribution towards preserving or enhancing the character or appearance of any conservation area. Applications should fall into one of the following categories:

- They are for works to a building in a conservation area of particular architectural or historic interest, for which the local authority has been invited by English Heritage to submit a programme of conservation work.
- There is a town scheme in operation in the same part of the conservation area as the application site.
- They are for a scheme of conservation work prepared by local authorities, amenity societies, preservation trusts or a group of private owners, for example a scheme for the restoration of buildings in a particular square, terrace, street or village. The individual grants sought could be for relatively small sums provided that they are part of a scheme. There are occasions when a grant for one building of particular interest can be the catalyst for further action in the locality. (To be accepted as a scheme, the total of the grants for the properties included in it must amount to £2,500 or more, ie £10,000 of work).
- They are for repair of buildings which have been the subject of notices under S. 101 or 115 of the Town and Country Planning Act 1971, especially if these buildings have been acquired by a local preservation trust for the specific purpose of restoration.

Eligible items for all S. 10 grants are assessed by English Heritage's architects but normally include structural repairs to the fabric of the building, repairs using natural or traditional materials, or restoration of features of historical or architectural interest.

Although priority is given to work on buildings, environmental works are considered for grant aid if they are in the vicinity of grant-aided schemes and if funds are available. Section 10 grants can exceptionally be given towards the cost of acquisition by a non-profit-making body of a building when this is for the express purpose of saving a building which would otherwise be lost.

Town scheme grants

Town scheme grants may be given under S. 10B of the 1972 Act. A town scheme is an arrangement whereby the Commission and local authorities concerned conclude a repair grant agreement setting aside matching sums for grants for buildings within an agreed area, which must be within a conservation area. Both statutorily listed buildings and unlisted buildings forming part of the townscape or having group value may be included in a scheme. The intention of grants is normally to carry out comprehensive repair of the historic buildings concerned. Only structural repairs are eligible, usually to external features, although internal work can be accepted if it stems from structural repairs to the exterior or is vital to the preservation of the structure.

Most town schemes are in fact administered by the local authority, although English Heritage does still administer some. In the first instance prospective applicants should contact their local authority.

Further information from:
English Heritage
Historic Areas Division
25 Savile Row
London W1X 2BT
(01) 734 6010 ext. 861
For S. 3A grant aid: ext. 882
For town scheme and S. 10 grant aid: ext. 861

Architectural Heritage Fund
The Architectural Heritage Fund, which is an independent charity, provides loan capital for local building preservation trusts or other charities which are restoring old buildings. Loans may be for up to 50 per cent of the gross cost of a project and are normally offered for a period of two years at 5 per cent per annum.

Further information from:
The Secretary
Hilary Weir
The Architectural Heritage Fund
17 Carlton House Terrace
London SW1Y 5AW
(01) 925 0199

Ancient Monuments

The Ancient Monuments and Archaeological Areas Act 1979 contains a number of grant-giving sections. Local authorities have similar powers. The relevant sections are:
- Grants can be given to individuals or organisations for the acquisition, preservation, management, or removal to a safe place of an ancient monument (S. 24)
- Grants can be given towards the costs of an archaeological excavation and publication of the results (S. 45)
- The DoE, Historic Buildings and Monuments Commission for England (English Heritage) and local authorities can enter into a wide variety of management agreements with the occupants of land on which an ancient monument is sited (S. 17).

In England, the first approach should be made to English Heritage, Ancient Monuments Division or the local authority.

Churches still in use are not eligible for grants through this legislation. In the cast of 'useful' buildings, such as a barn, windmill or occupied house, the first approach should be made to the Historic Buildings Division of English Heritage.

Further information from:
Ancient Monuments Division
Fortress House
23 Savile Row
London W1X 2HE
(01) 734 6010 ext. 434

FOREIGN AND COMMONWEALTH OFFICE

The Foreign and Commonwealth Office makes grants to a small number of voluntary organisations, e.g. the International Committee of the Red Cross and the Ockenden Venture, which are channelled through the Overseas Development Administration (see entry on page 27). There is no specific fund to which organisations not already in receipt of FCO grants may apply.

Further information from:
Foreign and Commonwealth Office
Government Offices
King Charles Street
London SW1A 2AH
(01) 270 3000

DEPARTMENT OF HEALTH

The DoH has a number of direct grant-giving schemes, mostly under S. 64 of the Health Services and Public Health Act 1968. In addition, there are special arrangements which enable voluntary organisations to obtain central government funds via health and local authorities (joint finance). Health authorities and local authority social service departments can also make grants to voluntary organisations out of their own funds.

DoH Direct Grants

Section 64 general scheme
The general scheme under S. 64 of the Health Services and Public Health Act 1968 provides grants to voluntary organisations. The major use of these

funds is to provide assistance towards the central costs of running a voluntary organisation whose work is national in scope, and thus give it a stable base. Grants could also be used for innovative projects which provide a particularly effective way of developing services of current importance to the DHSS.

Grants towards the central costs of a voluntary organisation can be made for up to three years and are renewable on review. For projects, commitments can be made for three years, and are not renewable. Applications for funding in the fourth year might be considered to allow the results of the project to be written up and disseminated. These grants are intended to assist voluntary organisations and will normally provide less than half the funding for an organisation or project.

The total DHSS expenditure on grants to voluntary organisations under the general scheme was £14.4 million in 1987/88.

Further information about the S. 64 general scheme is contained in notes for guidance and application forms available from:
Morton Phillips
Branch CS4C
DoH
Alexander Fleming House
Elephant and Castle
London SE1 6BY
(01) 407 5522 ext. 6003 or 7068

Grants to voluntary children's homes and assisted community homes
Capital grants can be made to voluntary organisations for the improvement of children's homes registered by the DoH, and for the improvement of assisted community homes under S. 82 of the Child Care Act 1980.

Further information from:
Mrs M Vallance
Branch CS2(c)
DoH
Alexander Fleming House
(01) 407 5522 ext. 7387

Opportunities for Volunteering
The Opportunities for Volunteering scheme was set up to increase opportunities for unemployed people to do voluntary work in the health or personal social services fields. The sum of £5.5 million is allocated under the scheme but the consortium's funds are fully committed until March 1992. The scheme is administered by 15 specialist agencies and a general fund compris-

ing seven national general voluntary bodies including NCVO. The general fund was intended to give funds to smaller voluntary bodies.

Further information from:
Consortium Co-ordinator
c/o NCVO
26 Bedford Square
London WC1B 3HU
(01) 580 6387

New Initiatives

The government also directs additional resources towards the voluntary sector through specific grants for particular initiatives: including intermediate treatment and day care for under-fives. Most of these will make use of S. 64 powers, although they will have separate budgets. Some schemes, however, like those for the mentally handicapped which involve the moving of children out of hospitals, will qualify for grants under joint finance (see below).

Intermediate Treatment Fund
The Intermediate Treatment Fund is administered by the Rainer Foundation through a special Fund Committee. It provides capital grants to assist with the provision of equipment and premises for IT activities and revenue grants to assist new projects with their first year running costs.

Further information from:
Intermediate Treatment Fund
33 King Street
London WC2E 8JD
(01) 379 6171

or

Branch ICS 2(B)
DoH
Alexander Fleming House
(01) 407 5522 ext. 6467

Day care for under-fives
The sum of £350,000 is being made available in 1988/89 to enable selected national voluntary bodies to give small grants to local groups for work with under-fives. These grants are for specific items such as equipment and not for long-term funding.

Further information from:
Colin Startup
Branch CS3C
DoH
Alexander Fleming House
(01) 407 5522 ext. 6130

Joint Finance

Under joint finance arrangements money is allocated each year to health authorities to support selected personal social services spending by local authorities or voluntary organisations. The aim is to encourage joint planning and collaboration between the authorities and voluntary organisations and to promote the development of community care. Voluntary organisations can qualify for grants under this scheme.

Voluntary organisations can receive joint finance directly from district health authorities (DHAs) or via local authorities. All joint finance schemes must be recommended by the local Joint Consultative Committees (JCCs). There are three representatives of voluntary organisations on these committees.

Normally grants made towards the capital costs of a jointly financed project should not exceed two-thirds of the total cost. The full running costs of a project can be met for up to three years, and support must cease after seven years, except where special circumstances arise which could not have been foreseen at the outset and the Secretary of State grants an extension for a maximum of two years more.

In 1988/89, some £113 million will be channelled through regional health authorities (RHAs) to DHAs to be spent under the joint finance fund.

The proportion of the allocated funds available for voluntary organisations' use is not fixed. The amount of this money going to voluntary organisations amounted to some £14 million in 1986/87.

Voluntary organisations applying for joint finance should initiate proposals and open discussions with their district health authority and/or local authority social services department, not approach the Department of Health.

District health authorities can make other grants to voluntary organisations working in the health and social services. Most of their support to voluntary organisations, though, comes through joint finance (see above) or partnership and programme funds (see DoE on page 15).

Care in the Community
This initiative has the specific aim of helping long-stay hospital patients unnecessarily kept in hospital to return to the community where it will be best for them, and is what they and their families would prefer.

Health authorities can make continuing payments from their normal funds to local authorities and voluntary organisations for 'identified' people moving into community care.

Joint finance is available on extended terms if necessary to help initiate such projects. This means it can be used to meet 100 per cent of the cost of the project for up to 10 years, and for 13 years in all.

Voluntary organisations applying for joint finance should initiate proposals and open discussions with their district health authority and/or local authority social services department, not approach the Department of Health.

Further information from:
CS4 Division
Room B1208
Alexander Fleming House
(01) 407 5522 ext. 7874

HOME OFFICE

Grants for voluntary organisations from the Home Office can be divided into four main categories:
- Voluntary Services Unit grants
- marriage guidance councils
- rehabilitation and after-care of offenders
- probation and bail hostels

Voluntary Services Unit

The Home Office Voluntary Services Unit (VSU) acts as a link between voluntary organisations and the government. It has both advisory and funding functions.

Advice
The VSU will advise an organisation on whether it might be eligible for a grant from central government and, if so, which department it should approach. It will also help any voluntary organisation trying to establish which part of the government might be interested in its work. The VSU tries to co-ordinate the response of different government departments to voluntary organisations and has liaison officers in a number of departments.

Funding
The VSU can fund organisations whose work is not the responsibility of a single government department. Normally these organisations will be working at a national level. The VSU can fund local projects which are innovatory and of national significance, if their work crosses department boundaries.

The type of organisation funded by the VSU includes those which are concerned mainly with the servicing of other voluntary organisations covering a wide variety of work and those recruiting volunteers to work in different services. Examples include the National Council for Voluntary Organisations, the Volunteer Centre, Community Service Volunteers, the Community Projects Foundation and the National Federation of Community Organisations.

The VSU can, in special circumstances, fund organisations in cases where there is currently no power for assisting a voluntary organisation but where there is good reason to believe funds will become available in the near future.

From time to time the VSU promotes specific funding initiatives for a limited period. Recent examples have included the Local Development Agencies Development Fund and money to assist the establishment of a number of community trusts.

In 1987/88, grants from the VSU to voluntary organisations totalled almost £10.2 million. Applications can be made to the VSU at any time of the year.

Organisations in Scotland and Northern Ireland can apply to the VSU, but funding is more limited than in England and Wales because of differences in the way responsibilities are allocated between government departments, and the financial arrangements which govern its funding.

Organisations in Scotland and Northern Ireland should apply in the first instance to the Scottish Office or Northern Ireland Office.

Further information from:
Voluntary Services Unit
Home Office
50 Queen Anne's Gate
London SW1H 9AT
(01) 273 2728

Marriage Guidance Councils

The Home Office makes grants to five organisations concerned with marriage guidance work. There is no pool of money for new applications – the available funds (£1,381,000 in 1987/88) are distributed among the Catholic Marriage Advisory Council, Family Welfare Association, the Tavistock Institute of Marital Studies, Jewish Marriage Guidance Education Council and RELATE (National Marriage Guidance).

Rehabilitation of Offenders

The Home Office makes grants to organisations engaged in the rehabilitation of offenders. Most of the money goes to organisations providing hostels or similar accommodation schemes in which places are reserved for offenders, and some 325 projects of this sort currently receive support. The remainder is used to support organisations which provide other forms of help to ex-offenders.

Any project receiving a grant must have the support of the local probation service and be run in consultation with that service.

Grants are made under S. 52(3)(f) of the Powers of Criminal Courts Act 1973, and about £620,000 has been made available in 1987/88. In addition the National Association for the Care and Resettlement of Offenders (NACRO) receives a grant-in-aid towards its central administration costs (£722,000 in 1987/88).

Further information from:
Stephen Gorman
C6 Division
Home Office
Room 430
50 Queen Anne's Gate
London SW1H 9AT
(01) 278 3104

Probation and Bail Hostels

The Home Office funds hostels for people on probation and bail who are required to stay in approved accommodation. These hostels are managed either by voluntary groups or the area Probation Service.

Further information from:
Wayne Ferguson
C6 Division
Home Office
50 Queen Anne's Gate
London Sw1H 9AT
(01) 213 5916

Work with Commonwealth Immigrants

The Home Office can provide grants of up to 75 per cent to local authorities under Section 11 of the Local Government Act 1966 for paying staff involved in meeting the special needs of immigrants from the Commonwealth whose language or customs differ from the rest of the community. Section 11 grant aid is used to fund a wide range of work concerned with the special needs of ethnic minorities.

Section 11 money can be used to fund 'detached duty' posts based within voluntary organisations. However, the post must remain a local authority post, accountable to a local authority manager, although the voluntary organisation can manage the post on a day-to-day basis.

You need to approach your local authority to see if they can apply for Section 11 funding from the Home Office for such a post in your organisation. However, it is important to think through working relationships for detached duty posts well in advance, and to negotiate mutually acceptable arrangements with the local authority, otherwise problems could result. For further information on all aspects of Section 11 see NCVO's guidance notes, *Section 11 – Funding for Black and Ethnic Minorities?*

The Home Office is currently introducing a scrutiny review of Section 11 which could result in changes during 1989 or 1990.

LORD CHANCELLOR'S DEPARTMENT

The Lord Chancellor's Department currently provides grants for seven law centres and the Law Centres Federation (£712,000 in 1987/88). There are no spare funds for new grants. The department does not make any other grants to voluntary organisations.

Further information from:
Lord Chancellor's Department
Trevelyan House
Great Peter Street
London SW1P 2BY
(01) 210 8500

OVERSEAS DEVELOPMENT ADMINISTRATION

The ODA is a functional wing of the Foreign and Commonwealth Office.

Joint Funding Scheme

The purpose of the Joint Funding Scheme (JFS) is to help British voluntary agencies extend their work among the poor in developing countries through financial support for specific developmental projects. Projects which would be eligible for support include those aimed at increasing production, improving skills and leading to better employment and income prospects, non-formal education, community health and family planning. Funds are not available for relief or welfare projects nor for conventional education or conventional curative medical projects.

The Overseas Development Administration will meet 50 per cent of the costs of a project. In the case of family planning projects, the ODA will consider meeting up to 100 per cent of the project costs.

To be eligible for support an agency must be a British non-governmental non-profit-making organisation. It must be registered as a charity and get its main income in the UK.

In 1988/89, £10.7 million has been allocated for the Joint Funding scheme. Of this, £6.1 million has been set aside for projects which will be undertaken by the ODA's major co-financers who are Oxfam, Christian aid, the Save the Children Fund and the Catholic Fund for Overseas Development (CAFOD). The remaining £1.5 million will be available for applications from other agencies.

Further information from:
Mr P Little
Room AH 169
Overseas Development Administration
Abercrombie House
Eaglesham Road
East Kilbride
Glasgow G75 8EA
(03552) 41199 ext. 3199

British Volunteers

The Overseas Development Administration supports four independent recruitment agencies to send suitably qualified volunteers for service overseas in response to requests from developing countries. The four organisations are:
- Voluntary Service Overseas
- Catholic Institute for International Relations
- International Voluntary Service
- United Nations Association International Service

ODA meets 90 per cent of the cost of the societies' volunteer programmes (including UK headquarters' costs) and the balance is met by the societies through their own fund-raising efforts.

Grants totalling £10.8 million have been agreed for the volunteer sector for 1988/89.

Further information from:
Mr A McSkimming
Room AH 169
Overseas Development Administration
Abercrombie House
Eaglesham Road
East Kilbride
Glasgow G75 8EA
(03552) 41199 ext. 3199

Disaster Unit

This unit is responsible for the government's response to any disaster in a developing country and to natural disasters in developed countries.

The unit has no fixed annual budget.

Much of the unit's expenditure is channelled through British voluntary agencies.

The unit also allocates up to £20,000 a year towards the administrative expenses of the Disasters Emergency Committee's secretariat. (The Disasters Emergency Committee comprises the British Red Cross Society, CAFOD, Christian Aid, Oxfam and the Save the Children Fund.)

Further information from:
R B Emery
Disaster Unit
Overseas Development Administration
Eland House
Stag Place
London SW1E 5DH
(01) 273 0273

Refugee Projects

Money is available for British voluntary agencies running projects providing relief assistance to refugees in developing countries.

Further information from:
Mrs Janette Wyeth
Overseas Development Administration
(01) 273 0253

Further information about the Overseas Development Administration and funding schemes for which a contact is not given:
Overseas Development Administration
Eland House
Stag Place
London SW1E 5DH
(01) 273 3000

DEPARTMENT OF TRADE AND INDUSTRY

Section 20 of the Competition Act 1980 enables the Secretary of State to make grants to bodies which advise him on matters of interest to users of goods and services, and which disseminate information and advice on such matters.

There are currently four voluntary organisations receiving grant aid under this heading, the major being the National and Scottish Associations of Citizens Advice Bureaux which between them received £9.3 million in 1988/89.

Further information from:
R W Insley
Consumer Affairs Division
Department of Trade and Industry
10–18 Victoria Street
London SW1H 0NN
(01) 215 3298
(01) 215 7877 (switchboard)

DEPARTMENT OF TRANSPORT

The Department of Transport makes very few grants to voluntary organisations and there is no specific fund to which organisations can apply.

Grants are given to organisations for road safety work, including the Royal Society for the Prevention of Accidents which received £530,000 in 1987/88.

The Department of Transport also funds the National Advisory Unit for Community Transport (£98,000 in 1988).

Further information from:
Ann Frye
Disability Unit
Department of Transport
Room S10/21
2 Marsham Street
London SW1P 3EB
(01) 276 5255

2
Grants from Organisations Authorised to Allocate Government Money

ARTS COUNCIL OF GREAT BRITAIN

The Arts Council is the principal channel for public subsidy of the arts. It receives an annual grant-in-aid from the government: the cash grant for the year ending 31 March 1989 is £150 million (including £23 million abolition replacement funding). From these funds the Arts Council provides financial support for arts organisations, artists, performers and others through a multiplicity of schemes.

Type of Grant

The grants made by the council fall into four categories:
(i) Revenue grants to established arts companies and organisations. These range from large sums like £7,811,400 for the National Theatre through to £64,525 for the Women's Theatre Group.
(ii) Grants and guarantees for specific projects. Examples include a £12,000 grant to the Theatre de Complicité for a mime project.
(iii) Bursaries and awards to composers for commissions, designers, artists in residence schemes, and arts training schemes.
(iv) Under the Art Development Strategy launched by the 'Glory of the Garden' report in March 1984, the council has made available some £3 million in 'challenge' funding to the local authorities for entirely new projects.

Generally, grants under category (i) are made only to organisations which have previously received a subsidy. However, categories (ii) and (iv) are available to companies and organisations with a track record of work against which they may be assessed. Grants and bursaries in category (iii) may be made direct to individual artists and performers, or they may be channelled through a 'host' organisation.

The council funds the Scottish and Welsh Arts Councils which operate along similar lines, but with a high degree of autonomy. The council is also the principal funding source for the 12 English regional arts associations (see entry on pages 43-44).

Further information (including directories and leaflets about specific areas of work, projects, awards, and schemes), from:
Information and Research
Arts Council of Great Britain
105 Piccadilly
London W1V 0AU
(01) 629 9495

BRITISH FILM INSTITUTE

The institute promotes the study and appreciation of the art of the film and television, and will consider relevant applications for funding. It is not the status of the body, but the purpose of the request which will determine the outcome of any application.

Examples of projects which may be grant aided are:
- financing of the production, distribution and exhibition of independent films or videotapes
- financial aid to organisations committed to raising the level of knowledge and understanding of film and television

Further information from:
British Film Institute
21 Stephen Street
London W1P 1PL
(01) 255 1444

BRITISH LIBRARY

The British Library Research and Development Department can award grants for research projects related to library and information operations in all subject fields. This support is directed to the benefit of the national library and information system as a whole. A statement on current research priorities is available. In 1987/88, approximately £1.5 million was expended on research projects, and 132 new research grants were awarded. All projects result in research reports which are made widely available, for purchase or loan.

The British Library can also award grants to libraries and similar institutions to conserve, catalogue and make accessible collections of national importance. In 1985 the Wolfson Foundation and Family Trust generously gave the Library £1 million spread over four years for the award of grants to other libraries specifically for the purchase and restoration of books and manuscripts.

The British Library also administers the Public Library Development Scheme on behalf of the Office of Arts and Libraries and the British National Bibliography Research Fund. A twice yearly Research Bulletin and a catalogue of publications are available free of charge from the Research and Development Department.

Further information from:
The British Library
Research and Development Department
2 Sheraton Street
London W1V 4BH
(01) 323 7060

COMMISSION FOR RACIAL EQUALITY

The CRE can fund any organisation which in its opinion is concerned with the promotion of equal opportunity and good relations between people from different racial groups.

Type of Grant

The scheme through which the commission can provide grants to voluntary organisations is Project Aid. The scheme applies throughout the United Kingdom. The closing date for applications for the *next* financial year is 31 October.

Applications which meet regional criteria stand a better chance of receiving funds.

Project Aid

Within this scheme, funds are disbursed for
(i) Short Term Grant Aid (STGA)
(ii) Long Term Grant Aid (LTGA)
STGA is a grant to a project whose planned life is less than two years and LTGA is a grant to a project whose planned life is two years or more. In all cases, grant aid will be initially considered on a one-year basis, and will be subject to review.

Grants are intended for pump priming in preparation for alternative funding. Permanent funding is not available. In both cases, grants can cover salaries, administrative and running costs and some materials and equipment. Where a grant is approved on a long-term basis, some capital costs (though purchase of land or premises is not included) and professional fees may also be considered.

In 1987, 207 applications were approved under Project Aid totalling just over £2.2 million.

At the time of going to press, the CRE's fund-raising strategy is under review.

Further information from:
The Field Services Division
Commission For Racial Equality
Elliot House
10–12 Allington Street
London SW1E 5EH
(01) 828 7022

COUNTRYSIDE COMMISSION FOR ENGLAND AND WALES

The commission is concerned with:
- the provision and improvement of facilities for the enjoyment of the countryside
- the conservation and enhancement of the natural beauty and amenity of the countryside
- the need to secure public access to the countryside for the purposes of open-air recreation

The commission recognises the valuable contribution voluntary bodies can make to conserving the countryside, and to recreation and access. Grants and other assistance are available for voluntary organisations whose main objectives are consistent with the commission's own objectives.

Countryside Grants for Voluntary Organisations

Grants are available to voluntary organisations for a variety of activities:
- Countryside Project Grants for acquiring land and running practical projects
- Countryside Information and Training Grants for running advisory, publicity and training activities
- Countryside Volunteer Grants for managing and supporting volunteers in the field
- Countryside Initiative Grants for expanding and developing voluntary organisations
- Countryside Low Cost Grants. These are available instead of the above four grants for all activities (except land acquisition) costing under £1,500 in total

Grants cannot be made retrospectively for work already undertaken. The maximum grant is limited to 75 per cent of eligible costs (excluding other government grants). However, grants above 50 per cent are exceptional.

A booklet, *Countryside Grants for Voluntary Organisations CCP 219*, is available from Countryside Commission Publications, 19–23 Albert Road, Manchester M19 2EQ.

Further information from:
Central Offices
John Dower House
Crescent Place
Cheltenham
Glos GL50 3RA
(0242) 521381

Warwick House
Grantham Road
Newcastle upon Tyne
NE2 1QF
(091) 232 8252
Northern

Ladywell House
Newtown
Powys SY16 1RD
(0686) 626799
Wales
Regional Offices

Terrington House
13–15 Hills Road
Cambridge CB2 1NL
(0223) 354462
Eastern

30–32 Southampton Street
London WC2E 7RA
(01) 240 2771
Greater London & South East

Cumberland House
200 Broad Street
Birmingham B15 1TD
(021) 632 6503
Midlands

Bridge House
Sion Place
Clifton Down
Bristol BS8 4AS
(0272) 739966
South West

8A Otley Road
Headingly
Leeds LS6 2AD
(0532) 742935
Yorkshire & Humberside

184 Deansgate
Manchester M3 2WB
(061) 833 0316
North West

Groundwork Foundation
Bennetts Court
6 Bennetts Hill
Birmingham B2 5BT
(021) 236 8565

There is a separate Commission for Scotland:
Countryside Commission for Scotland
Battleby
Redgorton
Perth PH1 3EW
(078) 27921

CRAFTS COUNCIL

The function of the Crafts Council is to support the crafts in England and Wales, and to promote the work of artist craftsmen and women.

The Crafts Council offers both business advice and finance to artist craftsmen and women as well as subsidy for craft projects. Details of the advice available and the different schemes are set out in the leaflet 'Grants, Loans and Business Advice'.

Further information from:
Grants and Services Section
Crafts Council
8 Waterloo Place
London SW1Y 4AU
(01) 930 4811

EQUAL OPPORTUNITIES COMMISSION

The EOC has a budget which it can make available to voluntary organisations or individuals for projects which fall within its own terms of reference. It is not sufficient for the project to benefit women. It must be a project which either helps to eliminate sex discrimination or promotes equality of opportunity between men and women. A group presenting a project for funding should therefore try to highlight how the project fulfils one or other of these objects.

The budget is divided under two headings:

Grants for Research and Educational Projects

Grants are normally made for a one-year period only. The EOC is reluctant to get involved in long-term funding because of its very limited grants budget. The types of project funded tend to incorporate new ideas or to look at problems in new ways. Grant applications exceeding £10,000 will rarely be successful, nor applications where a full-time salary for more than one worker is requested.

In 1987/88, £56,500 was available. There was, as usual, a heavy demand for this money: 135 applications were received for consideration and only 17 of those projects could be supported. Potential applicants should contact the EOC for details of closing dates.

Recent grants include:
- *National Council for One-Parent Families (London)* – £3,000 was awarded to impart financial training and expertise to individual one-parent families in an effort to create greater self-help among lone parents.

- *Family Welfare Association (Northampton)* – £3,500 was awarded to promote equal opportunities between men and women of the Asian communities.

The EOC does not normally cover capital expenditure on buildings or equipment, provide individual education or travel grants, support projects likely to have only local impact, make any kind of retrospective grant or consider re-applications within any 12 month period.

Grants for Conferences/Seminars

Applications for grants for conferences are considered throughout the year. They must be received by the commission no less than eight weeks before the date of the event. Decisions can usually be made within six weeks. Grants are relatively small, usually less than £500.

Applicants are advised to contact the EOC Voluntary Organisations Liaison Unit to discuss ideas before making an application.

Further information from:
Voluntary Organisations Liaison Unit
Equal Opportunities Commission
Overseas House
Quay Street
Manchester M3 3HN
(061) 833 9244 exts. 327, 329

There is a separate commission for Northern Ireland:
EOC for Northern Ireland
Lindsay House
Callendar Street
Belfast BT1 5DT
(0232) 42752

HEALTH EDUCATION AUTHORITY

The Health Education Council became the Health Education Authority in April 1987 with the status of a special health authority within the NHS. It provides limited grants for research projects.

Further information from:
Research Officer
Health Education Authority
Hamilton House
Mabledon Place
London WC1H 9TX
(01) 631 0930

HOUSING CORPORATION

The Housing Corporation is responsible for the funding, supervision and registration of housing associations in England. Housing associations are non-profit-making organisations run by a voluntary committee of management.

Type of Grant

Funds are available for the rehabilitation of older houses and new buidings. Grants meet the difference between the expenditure (on capital and interest) and income (rents, less management costs). Housing co-operatives are also eligible for funds.

A priority is funding of schemes to help people with special needs. This includes elderly people, physically or mentally handicapped people and hostel accommodation for single people.

The corporation is backing home ownership initiatives by housing associations designed to extend the range of housing available, through schemes such as shared ownership, leasehold for the elderly and improvement for sale.

The Housing Corporation's budget in 1988/89 is £737 million in England. Advice for new associations and co-operatives can be obtained from the appropriate regional office.

Further information from the Housing Corporation at:

Headquarters
149 Tottenham Court Road
London W1P 0BN
(01) 387 9466

Elisabeth House
16 St Peter's Square
Manchester M2 3DF
(061) 228 2951
North West: Cheshire, Cumbria, Greater Manchester, Lancashire

6th Floor
Corn Exchange Buildings
Fenwick Street
Liverpool L2 7RD
(051) 236 0406
Merseyside: Merseyside and West Lancashire, Warrington, Halton, Ellesmere Port and Neston District Councils

St Paul's House
23 Park Square South
Leeds LS1 2ND
(0532) 469601
North East: Cleveland, Durham, Humberside, Northumberland, Tyne & Wear, Yorkshire

Norwich Union House
Waterloo Road
Wolverhampton WV1 4BP
(0902) 24654
West Midlands: Hereford and Worcester, Salop, Staffordshire, Warwickshire, West Midlands

Phoenix House
16 New Walk
Leicester LE1 6TF
(0533) 546762
East Midlands: Cambridgeshire, Derbyshire, Leicestershire, Lincolnshire, Norfolk, Northamptonshire, Nottinghamshire, Suffolk

35a Guildhall Centre
Exeter EX4 3HL
(0392) 51052/4
West: Avon, Berkshire, Cornwall, Devon, Dorset, Gloucestershire, Hampshire, Isle of Wight, Oxfordshire, Somerset, Wiltshire

Waverley House
7–12 Noel Street
London W1V 4B4
(01) 434 2161
London and Home Counties (North): Bedfordshire, Buckinghamshire, Essex, Hertfordshire, London boroughs north of the Thames

Pembroke House
Wellesley Road
Croydon
Surrey CR9 2BR
(01) 681 3771
London and Home Counties (South): Kent, Surrey, Sussex, London boroughs south of the Thames

NATURE CONSERVANCY COUNCIL

The Nature Conservancy Council can award grants to individuals and organisations, public or private, for
- the establishment, maintenance and management of nature reserves in Great Britain
- the establishment of key posts within voluntary organisations to enable them to develop their nature conservation activities and, wherever possible, move towards financial self-sufficiency
- other innovative projects which further the practice of nature conservation
Applications will be assessed according to the expected direct benefits for nature conservation. Preference will be given to new projects, particularly those which will then lead on to further work. Grants are not given to subsidise organisations or finance deficits.

Volunteer Action Grants

Special arrangements have been introduced to encourage and increase the activity of volunteer members of county nature conservation trusts and other voluntary nature conservation bodies.

These grants can cover volunteers' expenses in carrying out an agreed programme of activities such as
- improvements in the management and maintenance of nature reserves
- practical arrangements to protect species
- measures which will increase an organisation's membership and financial resources
- increasing awareness and understanding of nature conservation

Only small amounts of money are available through this scheme.

Project Grants

These grants are for a wide range of practical projects of benefit to nature conservation. The grants are for projects costing over £200. Activities may include interpretative facilities for the education and enjoyment of visitors, and development of voluntary organisations.

Staff-post Grants

These grants help voluntary bodies to set up key posts, either full- or part-time.

There is no standard rate of grant but grants are normally up to 50 per cent of the agreed costs. Applications for grants can be made at any time but should be submitted at least three months before projects are due to start.

Further information from:
The Grants Officer
Nature Conservancy Council
Northminster House
Peterborough PE1 1UA
(0733) 40345

Direct enquiries about land purchase to the appropriate NCC country land agent:
NCC
Northminster House
Peterborough
England

NCC
12 Hope Terrace
Edinburgh EH9 2AS
(031) 447 4784
Scotland

NCC
Plas Penrhos
Ffordd Penrhos
Bangor
Gwynedd LL57 2LQ
(0248) 355141
Wales

REGIONAL ARTS ASSOCIATIONS

There are 12 regional arts associations. They are a source of advice and funding on the arts. Each employs a number of specialist officers, concerned with some or all of the following areas of arts activities: visual arts, craft, photography, drama, dance, music, film, video, television, literature, community arts, ethnic minority arts.

Voluntary organisations thinking of becoming involved with an arts project (particularly one concerned with the professional arts), which will involve them in any financial loss, are advised to discuss the project with the appropriate specialist officer at the nearest regional arts association.

Further information from:
Eastern Arts
Cherry Hinton Hall
Cherry Hinton Road
Cambridge
CB1 4OW
(0223) 215355

East Midlands Arts
Mountfields House
Forest Road
Loughborough
Leicester LE11 3HU
(0509) 218292

Greater London Arts
9 White Lion Street
London N1 9PD
(01) 837 8808

Lincolnshire and Humberside Arts
St Hugh's
Newport
Lincoln LN1 3DN
(0522) 33555

Merseyside Arts
Graphic House
107 Duke Street
Liverpool L1 4JR
(051) 709 0671

Northern Arts
10 Osborne Terrace
Newcastle upon Tyne NE2 1NZ
(0632) 816334

North West Arts
12 Harter Street
Manchester M1 6HY
(061) 228 3062

Southern Arts
19 Southgate Street
Winchester
Hampshire SO23 7EB
(0962) 55099

South East Arts
10 Mount Ephraim
Tunbridge Wells
Kent TN4 8AS
(0892) 515210

South West Arts
Bradninch Place
Gandy Street
Exeter EX4 3LS
(0392) 218188

West Midlands Arts
82 Granville Street
Birmingham B1 2LH
(021) 631 3121

Yorkshire Arts
Glyde House
Glydegate
Bradford
West Yorkshire BD5 0BQ
(0274) 723051

Scottish Arts Council
12 Manor Place
Edinburgh EH3 7DD
(031) 226 6051

Welsh Arts Council
Museum Place
Cardiff CF1 3NX
(0222) 394711

RURAL DEVELOPMENT COMMISSION

The Rural Development Commission is concerned to help alleviate economic and social problems in rural England. It supports the provision of workshops, small factory units, encourages the conversion of redundant buildings and through its Business Service provides professional and technical services to small rural businesses. The commission also supports the work of rural community councils and grant aids the Rural Unit of NCVO, and the headquarters work of the National Federation of Womens' Institutes. In its priority areas – the commission supports a wide range of projects designed to improve or maintain services or facilities which are not the main responsibility of other authorities, or which will benefit the economy of the area. In addition, grant aid is available directly for the following purposes:

Village Halls

Grants are available for the adaption or conversion of existing village halls to allow additional services or activities to be accommodated as long as they are new to that building. The purchase and/or adaption of redundant buildings (e.g. a school) to provide a community building in areas without any existing village hall is also eligible for grant.

Grants are only available in Rural Development Areas and the commission will pay up to 25 per cent of the cost, or £20,000 whichever is the lesser, on condition that there is some local authority contribution.

Local Enterprise Agencies

The commission contributes to the running of LEAs by a two-tier grant system aimed at helping small rural businesses to obtain professional help and advice. These are a Rural Project Grant (towards capital costs) and a Rural Activities Grant (towards financing professional advisers). Local Enterprise Agencies in rural areas are eligible to apply for grants.

TV Self-Help Schemes

Matching funds (up to £5,000) are available to help groups who want to set up their own transmitters where there is poor or non-existent TV reception. Groups must be formally constituted and have Home Office approval in principle before a grant can be considered.

Rural Transport

The commission operates the Rural Transport Development Fund with funds provided by the Department of Transport to encourage the provision of innovative projects to serve the transport needs of people living in rural areas where these are not already met, or likely to be met, by public transport services. The commission also provides a rural transport advisory service for existing and prospective operators.

Further information from:
The Rural Development Commission
11 Cowley Street
London SW1P 3NA
(01) 276 6969

SPORTS COUNCIL

The objects of the Sports Council are to foster the knowledge and practice of sport and physical recreation and to encourage the provision of sports facilities. The council makes the following grants to voluntary organisations in England:

(i) grants to the national governing bodies of sport for funding of development programmes within the body's forward plan (including drug testing)
(ii) grants to other national bodies with an interest in the promotion of sport and recreation
(iii) capital grants and interest-free loans to local voluntary organisations for the provision of local sports facilities
(iv) Regional Participation Grants for small, non-capital projects with the specific purpose of encouraging participation in sport
(v) both capital and revenue grants to support projects or schemes of wider than local significance in areas previously eligible for assistance by the GLC or metropolitan county councils

Most of these grants go to sports clubs. They are also available to youth organisations and other voluntary bodies for suitable sports projects.

In 1989/90 £9.825 million is budgeted for categories (i) and (ii). Under category (iii) some £3.5 million will be available in grants, £1.17 million in loans. Another £1.5 million and £3.4 million are allocated to categories (iv) and (v) respectively, although these grants are not restricted to voluntary organisations.

Examples of assistance given under category (iii) are
- £10,000 to a community association for the provision of changing rooms
- £2,000 grant and £3,000 loan to a village hall management committee for facilities for a village sports field
- £4,000 to a boys' club for the extension of premises to provide a sports hall

The Sports Council also administers a significant proportion of the Football Trust's grants programme for the improvement of football pitches and associated facilities.

Further information from:
For categories (i) and (ii)
The Sports Council
16 Upper Woburn Place
London WC1 0QP
(01) 388 1277

For categories (iii), (iv) and (v) contact the relevant regional office (see below), which will also give general and technical advice on the provision of sports facilities and the promotion of participation.

Aykley Heads
Durham DH1 5UU
(091) 384 9595
Northern Region: Northumberland, Cumbria, Durham, Cleveland, Tyne and Wear

Astley House
Quay Street
Manchester M3 4AE
(061) 834 0338
North West Region: Lancashire, Cheshire, Greater Manchester, Merseyside

Coronet House
Queen Street
Leeds LS1 4PW
(0532) 436443/4
Yorkshire and Humberside Region: W Yorkshire, S Yorkshire, N Yorkshire, Humberside

Grove House
Bridgford Road
West Bridgford
Nottingham NG2 6AP
(0602) 821887 and 822586
East Midland Region: Derbyshire, Nottinghamshire, Lincolnshire, Leicestershire, Northamptonshire

Metropolitan House
1 Hagley Road
Five Ways
Birmingham B16 8TT
(021) 456 3444
West Midlands Region: Metropolitan Authorities of the West Midlands, Hereford and Worcester, Shropshire, Staffordshire, Warwickshire

26 Bromham Road
Bedford MK40 2QD
(0234) 45222
Eastern Region: Norfolk, Cambridgeshire, Suffolk, Bedfordshire, Hertfordshire, Essex

PO Box 480
Crystal Palace National
  Sports Centre
Ledrington Road
London SE19 2BQ
(01) 778 8600
Greater London and South East Region: Greater London, Kent, Surrey, East and West Sussex

51A Church Street
Caversham
Reading RG4 8AX
(0734) 483311
Southern Region: Hampshire, Isle of Wight, Berkshire, Buckinghamshire, Oxfordshire

Ashlands House
Ashlands
Crewkerne
Somerset TA18 7LQ
(0460) 73491
South Western Region: Avon, Cornwall, Devon, Dorset, Somerset, Wiltshire, Gloucestershire

There are separate sports councils for Wales, Scotland and Northern Ireland. These have similar grant schemes to the English Sports Council.

Scottish Sports Council
1 St Colme Street
Edinburgh EH3 6AA
(031) 225 8411

Sports Council for Wales
National Sports Centre for Wales
Sophia Gardens
Cardiff CF1 9SW
(0222) 397571

Sports Council for Northern Ireland
2a Upper Malone Road
Belfast BT9 5LA
(0232) 381222

TOURIST BOARDS

The tourist boards of England, Wales and Scotland offer assistance for schemes to improve or provide tourist amenities and facilities.

Assistance can be offered in the form of either a grant or loan but is only available for schemes involving capital expenditure. The amount of grant or loan must not exceed half the total project cost.

The tourist boards produce their own literature on financial assistance for tourist projects. These can be obtained from the central offices or the appropriate regional board.

Further information from:
English Tourist Board
Thames Tower
Blacks Road
London W6 9EL
(01) 846 9000

Grants and Development
   Department
Thames Tower
Blacks Road
Hammersmith W6 9EL
(written enquiries only)

Wales Tourist Board
Brunel House
2 Fitzalan Road
Cardiff CF2 1UY
(0222) 499909

Scottish Tourist Board
23 Ravelston Terrace
Edinburgh EH4 3EU
(031) 332 2433

There are different criteria for funding tourist projects in Northern Ireland.

Information from:
Northern Ireland Tourist Board
River House
48 High Street
Belfast BT1 2DS
(0232) 231221/246609

Regional Tourist Boards

Cumbria Tourist Board
Ashleigh
Holly Road
Windermere
Cumbria LA23 2AQ
(096 62) 4444
(written enquiries only)
Cumbria

East Anglia Tourist Board
Toppesfield Hall
Hadleigh
Suffolk IP7 5DN
(0473) 822922
Cambridgeshire, Essex, Norfolk and Suffolk

Northumbria Tourist Board
Aykley Heads
Durham DH1 5OX
(091) 3846905
Cleveland, Durham, Northumberland, Tyne & Wear

North West Tourist Board
The Last Drop Village
Bromley Cross
Bolton
Lancashire BL7 9PZ
(0204) 591511
(written and telephone enquiries only)
Cheshire, Greater Manchester, Lancashire, Merseyside and the High Peak District of Derbyshire

Yorkshire and Humberside Tourist Board
312 Tadcaster Road
York
North Yorkshire YO2 2HF
(0904) 707961
North Yorkshire, South Yorkshire, West Yorkshire and Humberside

Heart of England Tourist Board
2–4 Trinity Street
Worcestershire WR1 2PW
(0905) 723394
(written and telephone enquiries only)
Gloucester, Hereford and Worcester, Shropshire, Staffordshire, Warwickshire and West Midlands

Thames and Chilterns Tourist Board
The Mount House
Church Green
Witney
Oxfordshire OX8 6DZ
(0993) 778800
Oxfordshire, Berkshire, Bedfordshire, Buckinghamshire and Hertfordshire

London Tourist Board and Convention Bureau
26 Grosvenor Gardens
London SW1W 0DU
(01) 730 3450
(written and telephone enquiries only)
Greater London

East Midlands Tourist Board
Exchequergate
Lincoln
Lincolnshire LN2 1PZ
(0522) 31521
(written and telephone enquiries only)
Derbyshire, Leicestershire, Lincolnshire, Northamptonshire and Nottinghamshire

South East England Tourist Board
1 Warwick Park
Tunbridge Wells
Kent TN2 5TA
(0892) 40766
East Sussex, Kent, Surrey and West Sussex

West Country Tourist Board
Trinity Court
37 Southernhay East
Exeter
Devon EX1 1QS
(0392) 76351
Avon, Cornwall, Devon, Dorset (parts of), Somerset, Wiltshire and Isles of Scilly

Southern Tourist Board
Town Hall Centre
Leigh Road
Eastleigh
Hampshire SO5 4DE
(0703) 616027
Hampshire, Eastern and Northern Dorset and Isle of Wight

TRAINING AGENCY

The Training Agency (formerly the Manpower Services Commission) is responsible for running the government's employment and training services. It runs a variety of schemes through which voluntary organisations can receive grants:
- Youth Training Scheme
- Employment Training
- Community Industry
- Sheltered employment and training schemes for the disabled

Youth Training Scheme

The two-year Youth Training Scheme (YTS) has been in operation since April 1986. The scheme offers a two-year training place to all 16-year-old school leavers whatever their employment status, and a similar offer of at least one year for all 17-year-old school leavers.

The objective of the scheme is to provide a foundation of broad-based vocational education and training and planned work experience, which gives all trainees the opportunity to obtain a vocational qualification related to competence in the work place or to obtain a credit towards such a qualification.

Young people must receive a minimum of 20 weeks off-the-job training over the two-year period.

Over the next few years each sector of industry and/or each occupational area will establish its own standards of competence. Any scheme offering training will have to conform to the newly established standards. At the same time new qualifications will be developed to reflect those standards.

Only 'approved training organisations' may take part in YTS. To achieve this status any voluntary organisation has to satisfy certain criteria relating to its resources, the competence of its staff, the suitability of its premises and equipment, its previous record in training and its financial stability.

The 1988 YTS funding review has developed a new funding structure for YTS to be implemented from April 1989. All YTS places will attract a management fee and a basic grant for each filled place on the scheme. Supplementary payments will be payable on top of the basic grant in standard units of equal value. The extra funding is meant to secure provision for young people with special training needs.

In 1986/87 some 270 voluntary organisations offered approximately 40,000 training places, about 10 per cent of the total provision. The continued involvement of voluntary organisations depends largely on their ability to attract funding from other sources. The government grant is meant only to be a contribution; employers are expected to provide their share of the costs.

Young people on the scheme are covered by a training agreement with the approved training organisation. This sets out the trainees' rights, responsibilities and their training programme. Trainees eligible for two years' training receive a minimum allowance of £29.50 in the first year of training and £35 in the second. Young people entitled to one year's training receive £29.50 per week for the first 13 weeks and £35 for the rest of the year. At these levels the allowances are exempt from income tax and national insurance.

The future shape of YTS and participation by voluntary sector providers will depend on decisions made by the local Training and Enterprise Council. A national network of 100 councils will be set up over the next four years to plan and deliver training at a local level.

Voluntary organisations wanting further information about YTS should contact their nearest Training Agency Area Office (number in the telephone directory) or

Tony White
Community Schemes Unit
NCVO
26 Bedford Square
London WC1B 3HU
(01) 636 4066

Employment Training

ET replaces the Community Programme, Voluntary Projects Programme, New Job Training Scheme and more than 30 other special employment measures formerly run by the Subcontractor. ET began on 5 September 1988. In its first year it aims to provide 300,000 places for training the long-term unemployed for future employment. In the second year the number of places on the scheme will remain the same, but the throughput of trainees is targeted at 600,000. On average trainees are expected to remain on the programme for six months, but there is the possibility for up to 12 months for some trainees. Participation in ET is on a full-time basis for most trainees, but again there is the option for some people with special needs to enter as part-time trainees.

Voluntary organisations will be directly responsible for between 30–40 per cent of all places in the first year, but the Training Agency (formerly the MSC) has made it clear that it intends to encourage private sector participation and that voluntary sector places will diminish over time. There is limited scope for ET providers to deliver benefits to the local community. The programme is mainly concerned with training individuals.

There are three ways for organisations to participate in the programme: as a Training Manager, a Training Agent, or a Subcontractor. The funding arrangements are different for all three.

An organisation becomes a Training Manager by submitting a bid (application) to its Training Agency Area Office. It does this in competition with all other organisations that also submit bids in its area. Each Area Office has a limited number of places to allocate and chooses the organisations that it considers best to operate the programme.

A Training Manager must ensure that each individual trainee receives appropriate training as outlined in their Individual Action Plan. A maximum of 60 per cent of a trainee's time is to be spent on practical on-the-job training, and at least 40 per cent on directed off-the-job training. A Training Manager can provide both elements of training directly or parts of it while subcontracting the rest to other organisations. A Training Manager is also responsible for arranging some work placement experience with an employer during each trainee's time on the programme.

If an organisation is successful in becoming a Training Manager it receives funds directly from the Training Agency on a filled-place basis. There is an initial single start-up payment of £15 per trainee; a weekly £17.50 grant for each full-time trainee; and for special needs or high-cost training places an additional weekly supplementary grant of between £0–£40, with an average place attracting £20. Training Managers must pay all of their fixed and variable costs from these revenues. Trainee allowances equal to their previous benefit plus an additional £10–12 is paid directly to them via Girocheque and is not the responsibility of the Training Manager.

An organisation can by itself or in a consortia bid to become a Training Agent. This is also done through bids to the local Area Office of the Training Agency. Training Agents counsel and advise prospective trainees about participation in ET, the local job market, and possible qualifications that can be obtained through entering ET. Each trainee is entitled to an Individual Action Plan that the Training Agent draws up for them which outlines the training to be provided by an appropriate Training Manager. The Training Agent is paid £20 per trainee assessment, with an additional £15 payment for each trainee that it successfully places with a Training Manager. The Training Agency suggests that a Training Agent will provide trainees with between 2-3 days of assessment, counselling and advice.

An organisation wishing to become an ET Subcontractor does not apply to or otherwise enter into any agreement or contract with the Training Agency. It does not receive any funds from the Training Agency. It must negotiate what is essentially a commercial contract with a Training Manager or Training Agent to provide a service. Training Managers may use Subcontractors to provide practical training, directed training, or both. Training Agents may use Subcontractors to provide trainees with special needs assessments. The financial arrangements for subcontracting are open for negotiation and no two agreements will be the same. It is up to the prospective Subcontractor to get the best deal from one or more Training Managers in its local area or even from another area. In principle a Subcontractor should aim to agree with a Training Manager or Training Agent a guarantee of a basic level of income that is sufficient to prevent any losses.

Recruitment to ET is for those who are aged at least 18 and under 60 and have been unemployed for six months, with a priority for those aged 18-24 who have been unemployed for between 6 and 12 months and for those aged 18-50 who have been unemployed for more than two years. Normally, trainees will be in receipt of benefit. They will be entitled to a training allowance equal to their benefit plus £10-12. Travel costs over £5 per week can be claimed and there is provision of bonus payments on a pro rata basis up to £250 for a 52 week period. Lone parents may claim up to £50 per week for childcare while on the programme.

Further information from:
Training Agency Area Offices or
Jobcentres

or

John Mabbott
Employment Unit/NCVO
26 Bedford Square
London WC1B 3HU
(01) 636 4066 ext. 2139

Community Industry

The Community Industry scheme aims to help particularly disadvantaged 16–19-year-olds find and keep work by providing them with temporary employment of benefit to the community. Most of the participants have left school with no qualifications. Special emphasis is placed on the personally and socially disadvantaged.

The scheme has been running since 1972, under the auspices of the National Association of Youth Clubs (NAYC). In 1984, Community Industry became a company limited by guarantee, with charitable status. Recently Community Industry has set up two subsidiary companies: Community Industry Youth Training and Community Industry Employment Training. Through a grant from the Department of Employment, Community Industry employs the permanent adult staff and young employees. The relevant authorities provide premises, transport and equipment. Community Industry teams work on projects and in workshops. The work undertaken must benefit the community and must be work which would not otherwise have been done. The range of work includes construction, painting and decorating, landscaping, and workshop activities – carpentry, metal-working and printing. The scheme also includes provision for training in social and life skills, literacy and numeracy.

Further information from:
Community Industry
24 Highbury Crescent
London N5 1RX
(01) 226 6663

Community Industry Employment
Training Agency Manager
Harbro House
Chapel Street
Okell Street
Runcorn
Cheshire WA7 5AP
(09285) 63153/63251

Sheltered Employment and Training Schemes for Disabled People

Sheltered employment

Sheltered employment is provided for severely disabled people who are unlikely, because of the severity of their disability, to obtain and retain a job except under special sheltered conditions.

Voluntary organisations and local authorities run sheltered workshops partly funded by the Employment Service of the Employment Department Group. The Employment Service contributes towards the running and capital costs of the workshops.

Employees work a normal week and produce goods or services which contribute substantially to the costs of the workshop. They receive wages and pay income tax and national insurance contributions in the normal way.

The Sheltered Placement Scheme is a fast expanding cost-effective and popular form of sheltered employment which allows severely disabled people to do ordinary jobs alongside able-bodied colleagues. There is a three-way agreement between a sponsor (which for legal reasons needs to be a voluntary organisation approved by the Employment Service, a local authority or Remploy Ltd), a 'host firm' which provides the work and workplace, and the Employment Service. The sponsor employs the severely disabled person who is paid the usual rate for the job. The 'host firm' pays the sponsor according to the amount of work the severely disabled person can do. The Employment Service, which approves schemes in the first place, pays the sponsor a grant to compensate for the difference between wages and other costs of employment, and the payment received from the host firm. Virtually all types of jobs can be done within the scheme.

Further information from:
Nearest jobcentre (addresses in the telephone directory) or:

Employment Department Group
Employment Service
Disabled People's Branch
Steel City House
Moorfoot, Sheffield S1 4PQ
(0742) 739190

Training provision for people with disabilities
Vocational training is available through the Training Agency's adult programme Employment Training.

Employment Training aims to help unemployed people gain the skills and experience they need to compete for jobs. The programme is open to people aged 18 and over who have been registered unemployed for 26 weeks. The standard eligibility rule of 6 months' unemployment can be relaxed for people with disabilities wishing to enter Employment Training.

The programme provides each trainee with an individually tailored training package which means that training can be linked to individual needs and abilities including the needs of those with disabilities. Wherever possible trainees with disabilities will train in integrated provision alongside non-disabled trainees using special help and additional funding where necessary. Specialist, possibly residential provision will be available for those who need it. Every training package includes an integrated mixture of practical and directed training.

Employment Training is delivered by Training Agents and Training Managers. The Training Agent helps the individual assess their training needs, explores the training opportunities available and draws up an action plan outlining the training to be undertaken. The Training Manager is responsible for arranging the agreed plan of training and practical experience for the trainee.

Features of Employment Training which may particularly assist people with disabilities are as follows:

- *Extended introduction* – people with disabilities who have doubt about their ability to cope with the programme will be eligible for an extended introduction period of up to 12 weeks with part-time attendance initially to enable them to sample the sorts of opportunities available locally. For the first 4 weeks participants will be able to remain on benefits, thereafter converting to ET allowances.
- *Part-time participation* – Employment Training has been designed primarily to offer full-time training to help people to take up full-time employment. However, part-time participation may be available to people with disabilities if their capacity to train full time is limited by their medical condition, provided that they are seeking to enter or re-enter the labour market.
- *Special help schemes* – as in YTS, a range of specific help for trainees with disabilities is available in the form of special aids to employment, adaptations to premises and equipment, a communicator service for deaf trainees and a personal reader service for blind trainees.
- *Special training provision* – where, exceptionally, people with disabilities are not able to enter local mainstream provision, or the costs of meeting their needs are such that they cannot be met through the grants available to Training Managers, the purchase of individualised opportunities will be funded under special arrangements within the programme.
- *Residential training* – residential training is available within Employment

Training for those trainees with disabilities whose needs are such that they can be best met through residential provision.

Information about Employment Training opportunities available in a local area is available form your local Jobcentre or local Training Agency Area Office.

YOUTH EXCHANGE CENTRE

The Youth Exchange Centre (YEC) was established on 1 April 1985 by the government to promote youth exchanges between the United Kingdom and other countries. It has the responsibility for the development, implementation and evaluation of policy governing youth exchanges and for advice on this to the government.

The YEC draws its staff and resources from the two publicly funded bodies, the British Council and the Central Bureau. The YEC administers grants for youth exchanges as well as providing information, advisory and training services, and is the national designated body administering the European Community 'Youth for Europe' exchange scheme.

Grants are available to British youth groups to assist with the costs, not only of travelling abroad, but also of hosting visiting youth groups to the United Kingdom. Priority is given to groups of young people, aged 16–20 (the groups must be aged between 14–25), engaged in two-way exchange projects emphasising social contact with the partner group.

Grants are available for youth exchanges with similar groups in Western Europe, Eastern Europe (including the USSR), the USA and Pakistan. Grants for exchanges with Commonwealth countries are administered by the Commonwealth Youth Exchange Council.

Full details are available in the information sheet: 'Guidelines to Applicants for Youth Exchange Grants'.

In addition, a limited fund is available to youth workers to improve the quality of international youth exchange through individual planning visits.

The YEC has established 12 Regional Committees throughout the UK which will be responsible for the provision of local information and training and for making decisions on YEC exchange grants for West Europe, Poland, Yugoslavia and the USA.

Further information from:
Youth Exchange Centre
Seymour Mews House
Seymour Mews
London W1H 9PE
(01) 486 5101

3
Money from Europe

EUROPEAN SOCIAL FUND

The European Social Fund (ESF) is the most important source of EEC funding for voluntary organisations. The purpose of the fund is 'to improve the employment opportunities for workers in the Common Market and to contribute thereby to raising the standard of living'. The fund supports the running costs of a number of vocational training and job creation schemes.

ESF grants only cover running costs (including items such as creche facilites). Capital costs, even if fundamental to a project, are not met. Costs such as renting premises and interest charges on a loan for a building can be included.

The European Social Fund was reviewed at the end of 1988. It is now expected to concentrate on programmes for people under 25 and for people out of work for more than six months. Applications have to be submitted through new 'partnership' committees which also monitor the work.

Further information and details of
application procedures from:
European Social Fund Unit
Department of Employment
11 Belgrave Road
London SW1V 1RB
(01) 834 6644

OTHER SOURCES OF EEC MONEY

There are other sources of money from Europe, but, as far as UK voluntary organisations are concerned, only relatively small amounts are available from each.

Grants for Research into European Integration

The EEC offers financial support to teachers, researchers and students engaged in studies and research on European integration.

Information and Education

Grants can be made to support information activities about the EEC, directed towards young people or adult education. The London Office of the European Commission can give information on jointly funded information activities.

If the information activity involves two or more EEC countries, the Commission in Brussels will consider making a grant to cover half the costs. Those interested should write to:

Directorate for Education, Vocational Training and Youth Policy
DG V
Commission of the European Communities
200 rue de la Loi
1049 Brussels

Aid to Coal and Steel Regions

Loans at low rates of interest are available towards improving the housing conditions of workers in coal and steel industries. Loans are available to public bodies and private organisations (including voluntary organisations) for the construction, purchase or modernisation of housing.

Aids for Research and Development

Funds are available for pilot projects with a European dimension concerned with research into problems faced by handicapped people (Helios Programme).

Human Rights

Grants are available to a limited extent for voluntary organisations promoting human rights and pursuing humanitarian aims.

Further information from:
Secretariat General of the
  Commission of the European
  Communities
200 rue de la Loi
1049 Brussels

Contact:
Bill Seary
NCVO
26 Bedford Suare
London WC1B 3HU
(01) 636 4066

A booklet *Finance from Europe: A guide to grants and loans from the European community* can be obtained from them free of charge. See also *Grants from Europe: How to Get Money and Influence Policy,* listed on page 79.
NCVO can provide advice about all aspects of money from Europe.

4
Grants from Local Authorities

BACKGROUND

Local authorities are a major source of funding for voluntary organisations. A survey carried out by the Charities Aid Foundation estimated that local authorities in the UK contributed £402.1 million to voluntary organisations in grants and fees in 1986/87, compared with £279.5 million in grants from central government in the same year.

However, local authority spending has been severely squeezed in recent years through rate-capping and grant penalties and has also faced a number of competing pressures as a result of time-expiry in the Urban Programme, tapering of the 'post-abolition' arrangements and loss of the Community Programme. It is therefore increasingly difficult to get grants for new projects.

A local authority has certain responsibilities – 'statutory obligations' – which it is obliged to meet. It has additional powers to fund projects which it decides will be of benefit locally. However, a local authority is not obliged to fund any particular voluntary organisation or to allocate any specified proportion of its budget to the voluntary sector. Similarly, if a grant has been given one year, the local authority does not normally have to continue the funding in future years. There are exceptions (see section on the Urban Programme, page 14).

Local authorities vary enormously in their attitude to the voluntary sector and in their interpretation of what is of local benefit. They also differ considerably in structure. Local authorities are organised in departments, each responsible to a committee of elected councillors. The main departments and committees likely to give grants to voluntary organisations include those dealing with social services, housing, education, planning, youth and community, and recreation and leisure; there may also be committees or sub-committees dealing with race, women's issues, employment or the Urban

Programme. Some local authorities have set up a central grants committee, perhaps as a sub-committee of the social services or policy and resources committee. Others have a grants unit and one or more grants officers to help with inquiries.

It is very important that you find out about the structure of your local authority and find out which committees give which kinds of funding. By tailoring your application in an appropriate way, you could get grants from different committees, or even get separate funding from several committees. It is also important to find out what criteria, guidelines and conditions are laid down by these committees. For example, some local authorities insist that an organisation has an equal opportunities policy, and many say that it cannot have relatives of paid workers on its management committee. The reasons for most criteria will be obvious; but voluntary organisations should be on the look-out for any conditions which restrict their independence.

Local authorities may give grants towards staffing and running costs (revenue expenditure) or towards premises or major items of equipment (capital expenditure). Since these two types of expenditure are controlled in different ways, they are likely to have different kinds of grant conditions attached to them. You should find out whether what you want is classified as revenue or capital expenditure.

As well as money, local authorities can provide premises, supplies and loans. Many local authorities employ staff whose responsibility is to work with the voluntary sector and who can provide advice about grants. These staff have a confusing array of titles: voluntary service co-ordinators, community development officers, link officers, voluntary organisations liaison officers, etc. Local councils for voluntary service or rural community councils, as well as other more specialised agencies such as law centres or cooperative development agencies, will be able to offer advice.

It is important for voluntary organisations to distinguish between 'arm's-length' funding for a voluntary activity and contractual payments for specific services rendered or functions fulfilled. In the case of 'arm's-length' support, voluntary bodies should accept reasonable accountability to establish the propriety of the expenditure but should not accept interferences in policy or operational matters (see Appendix 2).

In the case of contractual payments for services rendered, voluntary bodies should try to ensure that agreements are clearly written to establish precisely what the local authority is expecting; what forms of accountability will be required; and, before the contract is signed, judge whether these are practical and reasonable. NCVO has published a code for voluntary organisations entitled 'Relations between the Voluntary Sector and Government' (Appendix 2), which includes advice on these issues.

Before applying for local authority grants, then, you should find out about the local authority's structure and also about what kind of projects they are interested in funding. Some authorities will give priority to community care schemes or projects using volunteers; others to projects for women or ethnic minority groups or schemes providing employment.

Decisions are taken by local councillors. You should find out who the key councillors are and do some lobbying before your grant application is considered by the committee. The local authority officers make recommendations about grants to councillors. They will often help with drawing up applications and preparing budgets, and it is useful to have their support, too, as early on in the process as possible. The timetable for considering applications varies between authorities, but it is advisable to open discussions in early summer for a grant intended to begin the following financial year (i.e. from 1 April).

Getting your application right, establishing a good relationship with the officers dealing with your application and lobbying councillors are all important to the success of any grant application (see Appendix 1, 'How to Apply for a Grant').

LEGAL FRAMEWORK OF LOCAL GOVERNMENT

Voluntary organisations need not understand the entire complexities of local government's legal framework, but five aspects are especially important:

- the structure of local government and the different powers of counties, districts and boroughs
- arrangements in metropolitan areas
- where local authorities get their money
- local authorities' funding powers, including their discretionary powers
- rate relief

Structure of Local Government

The Local Government Act 1972 divided England and Wales (excluding Greater London) into counties which are themselves divided into districts. London has 32 boroughs, plus the City of London. There are 39 county councils and 296 district councils in England, 8 county councils and 37 district councils in Wales. In London and the metropolitan areas, most powers – including housing, social services and (except in Inner London) education – lie with district and borough councils. In the rest of the country – the 'shire' areas – district councils run housing, but education and social services are run by the county councils.

Some districts are also sub-divided into parishes in England and communities in Wales. There are more than 10,000 of such local councils in England and Wales. Only a few of these local councils currently give grants to local voluntary organisations.

The Local Government Act 1985 abolished 7 of the county councils – the Greater London Council (GLC) and the 6 metropolitan county councils (MCCs). The Act devolved some of their powers to the 32 London boroughs and the City of London and to the 36 metropolitan district councils, with effect from 1 April 1986. Other powers, e.g. for transport and fire, have passed to an array of countywide joint boards and committees.

The Education Reform Act 1988 abolished the Inner London Education authority (ILEA) with effect from 1 April 1990 and devolved responsibility for education to the inner London boroughs.

Arrangements in Metropolitan Areas

Funding arrangements in London, West Midlands, South Yorkshire, West Yorkshire, Greater Manchester, Merseyside and Tyne and Wear are more complex than other parts of the country. The individual boroughs and metropolitan districts will give grants on the same basis as other local authorities, although their budgets are often under particular pressure as a result of the commitments they inherited from the Greater London Council (GLC) and metropolitan county councils (MCCs). Initially the government provided 75 per cent grant aid (known as 'transitional finance') towards some of these commitments, but by 1989/1990 this has been reduced to 25 per cent, leaving the boroughs/districts with an increased burden to pay.

In addition the boroughs/districts have the power under S. 48 of the Local Government Act 1985 to establish cross-borough or countywide grant schemes. These have been established in all the metropolitan areas except South Yorkshire and Merseyside. Each scheme has its own priorities and procedures and the size of the schemes varies greatly. More detailed information should be obtained from the lead borough/district for the scheme.

In London, Richmond upon Thames is the lead borough for the London Boroughs Grants Scheme. The scheme's budget for 1988/89 was £28.5 million. The scope for funding new projects is limited because of existing commitments but in 1988/89 £1 million was identified for new developments. Apart from small one-off recurrent grants under £6,000, the scheme does not make any capital grants. To be eligible voluntary organisations' work must be London-wide in scope, or benefit more than one borough or constitute part of a London-wide pattern of provision.

S. 48 schemes are also operated in West Midlands (led by the City of Birmingham), Greater Manchester (City of Manchester), West Yorkshire (Wakefield Metropolitan District Council) and Tyne and Wear (South Tyneside MDC). However, in all four cases the scope for funding new revenue or capital projects is currently extremely limited. There are sometimes opportunities for obtaining one-off, non-recurrent revenue grants.

The Secretary of State for the Environment also has the power under S. 49 of the Local Government Act 1985 to establish trusts with money from the sale of the GLC and MCCs' assets. However, he has only used this power in London where the Trust for London was formed in 1986, and is managed by the City Parochial Foundation. The trust has an annual grants budget of up to £600,000 and aims to benefit and give priority to small local community-based organisations with charitable purposes. Initially there will be three distinct areas of work for which different procedures and timetables will apply:
- small grants for organisations in any borough, i.e. up to £500
- priority categories: black and ethnic minority groups and women's groups in any borough
- a four-year borough-based programme for local charitable organisations in eight named boroughs each year

Further information from:
Secretary
City Parochial Foundation
10 Fleet Street
London EC4Y 1AU
(01) 353 5678

There are also a number of joint boards in the metropolitan areas which have sometimes given grants to voluntary organisations operating in their area of concern. For example, London Regional Transport and Greater Manchester Transport Authority have funded Dial-a-Ride schemes and Merseyside Enterprise Board has funded employment and training projects. For further information about these possibilities contact the joint board direct or ask your local district or borough council for guidance.

Finally, following the Education Reform Act 1988, the Inner London Education Authority (ILEA) is to be abolished as from April 1990. Alternative arrangements for funding voluntary organisations supported by ILEA are currently under discussion. However, it is likely that projects covering more than one borough will be incorporated into the London Boroughs Grants Scheme arrangements and that local projects will have to look to their local borough.

Where Local Authorities Get their Money

Local authorities get their money from two main sources. They levy rates on local residents and businesses, and are given a general grant called Rate Support Grant (RSG) by central government.

Central government has argued that local authorities should spend less. It has set levels of spending for each authority, and where authorities have chosen to spend above this level central government has reduced the amount of RSG they get, using a system of penalties. Many local authorities have responded to RSG penalties by raising their rates. The Rates Act 1984 gave central government the power to set maximum rates – 'rate caps' – either by selecting a number of high-spending authorities (except those spending below a level set at £10 million for 1985/6 and limited to movements in overall planned spending together) or by capping all authorities' rates (with some possible exceptions). In 1985/6, 18 authorities were rate-capped, with 32 being capped in 1986/87, reaching a peak of 40 rate-capped authorities (which included 20 new joint boards) in 1987/88. By 1989/90, the number of rate-capped authorities had dropped to eight. This local government finance system affected voluntary organisations because it limited local authorities' ability to spend money on new grants, especially in the rate-capped areas.

The position was further complicated by abolition because central government's contribution to post-abolition funding was on a reducing scale, thus increasing the burden on local authorities each year. Time expiry in the Urban Programme (see page 14) and in special central government programmes has added further to this problem. In view of these difficulties, organisations seeking grants will need to find out enough about their own authority's position to understand – or even argue with – what officers and councillors say about their finances.

The future of local authority finances will be different from the arrangements described above. After 1990 (1989 in Scotland) domestic rates (that is, rates paid by householders) will be replaced by a flat-rate 'community charge' or poll tax which will be paid by virtually all adults. Non-domestic rates will in future be set by central government, pooled and redistributed to local authorities on the basis of their adult population. Rate Support Grant – including the system of penalties – will be replaced by a new Revenue Support Grant which is intended to be much simpler.

The introduction of the new system of finance will put considerable pressure on local authorities. Higher-spending councils, particularly in inner London, are expected to face very high local tax bills. Lower spenders, particularly in the Home Counties and the West Midlands, will see overall local tax bills reduced. Within every authority, the burden of paying for local government will shift away from ratepayers onto all adults, and will thus disadvantage all households with more than two adults. Large households (i.e. those with three or more adults) and homes where rate bills are currently low are likely to lose out. As the cost of local services moves in this direction, generally falling on poorer individuals, it will become harder for councillors to raise income.

Local Authorities' Funding Powers

Local authorities can only give grants to voluntary organisations when they have the power to do so. They cannot go beyond the limits that Parliament lays down for them through statute; to do so would be 'ultra vires'.

There are, in fact, a wide range of powers which local authorities can use to fund voluntary organisations and it is usually not the lack of power which might prevent an organisation getting a grant, but a lack of money or priority. Appendix 3 describes some of the main powers available and NCVO's own guide on the subject, *Getting in on the Act* (see page 79) gives further details.

Where a local authority does not have a specific power it can often use its discretionary funding powers under S. 137 of the Local Government Act 1972. S. 137 allows authorities to spend money on anything which they consider to be of benefit to their area – up to a maximum of the amount they raise from a 2p rate. Often authorities use this general power to fund new activities, such as work on unemployment or economic development. It is also used to fund services which are the responsibility of another tier of local government (e.g. a district council funding a local social services project). Some aspects of advice work and local development agencies work are also often funded under S. 137.

Some authorities have reached or nearly reached their 2p spending limit and this can sometimes be cited as a reason why an organisation cannot be funded. Very often in these cases there *are* alternative funding powers which could be used to relieve the pressure on S. 137, and details are given in the guide referred to above.

The government is currently in the process of amending S. 137. This is partly because abolition of the rates means that the 2p spending limit needs to be replaced with a new form of limit which does not depend on the rating system and partly because the Widdicombe Committee's Inquiry into the Conduct of Local Government Business was asked to examine the whole S. 137 system. The government's proposals are in the 1989 Local Government and Housing Bill, which proposes a new limit of £5.00 per head of adult population in areas where there is a single tier of local government (i.e. metropolitan areas) and £2.50 where there are two tiers. This provides for a total of approx £200 million spending in England and Wales compared with approx £300 million under the 2p limit. However, the government is also proposing a new economic development power in the same Bill. Since two-thirds of current S.137 spending is on economic development, this should ease the pressure on discretionary spending in most parts of the country.

Rate Relief

There is current mandatory rate relief of 50 per cent on rates for charities, while local authorities also have discretion to grant up to 100 per cent rate relief for voluntary organisations. Following the Local Government Finance Act 1988, charities in non-domestic properties (e.g. charity shops, day centres, training centres, etc.) will receive 80 per cent mandatory relief from the new non-domestic rate, which will be set by central government. Local authorities will also continue to have discretion to grant up to 100 per cent rate relief for voluntary organisations. Half the cost of this relief will be met through the community charge and the other half through non-domestic rate income.

Charities in domestic properties, where staff or clients are living on the premises (e.g. residential homes, hostels etc.) will be subject to the community charge system. However, most short-stay hostels run by voluntary organisations will be exempt. Rebates of up to 80 per cent will also be allowable under specific circumstances.

Detailed regulations covering the new system are currently being drawn up. The new system comes into force on 1 April 1990.

Richard Gutch
Assistant Director, Local Voluntary Action Department, NCVO

APPENDIX 1

How to Apply for a Grant

Voluntary organisations can apply for grants from central or local government, from trusts and charitable bodies and from industry. First you need to select the most appropriate source of funds. It is almost always worth contacting the grant-making body to ask questions, see what kind of approach they favour and discuss your application in draft form. This initial approach is essential in the case of large government departments, such as the Department of Health and local authorities, which offer many different grant schemes. It is not appropriate for a small trust which has no staff to answer telephone enquiries. An informal approach should be made to large trusts, however.

It is important to be absolutely clear about the purpose of the project for which you are seeking funds and how it meets the conditions of the grant. The Voluntary Services Unit at the Home Office (50 Queen Anne's Gate, London SW1H 9AT, (01) 273 2728) has consultants who are able to advise on the relevant central government department at which to direct the application to ensure it reaches the right target. Many local authorities have grants officers – often based in the social services department or the chief executive's office – who can give similar advice at the local level. If not, contact your local council for voluntary service and talk to other organisations who have succeeded in getting grants.

Some grant-giving bodies issue application forms while others require you to make your own presentation. In either case a concise, relevant and well argued application may be decisive in winning the donor's support.

If there is an application form, make sure you read it carefully before filling it in. If there is no form, it is useful to structure the application in such a way as to ensure that all aspects are properly covered, and that all the potential questions in the donor's mind are answered. A suggested structure is given below. Many of these points will also be equally relevant when filling in an application form. Very often these don't ask the type of questions which allow you to make your case, nor is enough space given for you to explain important matters. It is then best to put these under a general heading like 'additional information' on a separate piece of paper and clip it to the form.

Always keep a photocopy of the completed application form on file and always check that the funding agency has received the application. It also helps if one person is made responsible for the application so that the funding body knows who to contact.

Proposal summary
A clear concise and specific summary of your proposal will ensure maximum initial impact. This is best done in the form of a covering letter or an opening section of the introduction.

Introduction
It is important to say who you are and what are the aims and activities of the organisation. This is an opportunity to build your credibility and to convince the funding source that you are a viable and worthwhile recipient of funds. Press reports, letters of support from other agencies and clients, and statements from significant people testifying to the effectiveness of your work should be included if these are strictly relevant; but beware of providing too much back-up information.

Problem statement or assessment of need
It is important to spell out who are the people the proposal is intended to assist. Try to define as clearly and convincingly as possible the specific problem which needs funding for its solution – but don't overdo it by painting too lurid a canvas. Try to document the problem – but again avoid too much statistical overkill.

Programme objectives
Set out the objectives of your scheme and the outcome you hope for.

Methods
Set out what methods you will use and the activities you will conduct to accomplish your objectives. It may be useful at this point to bring in comparative information about other organisations which might have successfully employed the methods you are proposing – although the merit of your project may be that it is an entirely new approach. The more you say about your methods the more confidence you will inspire.

Evaluation
Say how you plan to evaluate the programme as this will be an indication of your determination to pursue the objectives effectively.

Budget
Make sure that the budget includes *all* overheads and that some allowances are made for inflation for each year for which the proposed scheme will run. The inflation rate may vary between different items, e.g. rent may not rise as much as staff salaries. Annual salary scale increments should be costed in over and above inflation. You must divide your budget into capital and revenue expenditure. Capital expenditure includes all one-off expenditure such as

altering premises or buying major equipment. Revenue expenditure includes all ongoing costs.

Here is a check-list:

CAPITAL

Acquisition of premises
Conversion of premises
Purchase of major equipment associated with the premises, e.g. telephone, office equipment, furnishings, fire preventing equipment, etc.
Purchase of other major equipment, e.g. vehicles, machinery, etc.

REVENUE

Salaries and on-going costs
Staff salaries
National Insurance contributions
Superannuation
Travel and subsistence for staff
Contingency fund for absent staff
Staff training
Volunteer expenses

Administrative
General insurance
Rent
Rates
Lighting
Heating
Cleaning
Maintenance
Telephone: rental
          calls
Printing/photocopying
Publicity
Affiliations/subscriptions
Stationery
Postage

Fees
Audit
Bookkeeping
Consultancy/specialist fees

Transport
Hire of vehicles
Insurance/road tax
Maintenance/servicing
Petrol

Equipment
Small replacement items

Evaluation costs

Miscellaneous

Note: you don't have to apply for all these items. Use them as a check-list so that major items don't get forgotten.

Future funding

If the programme is to continue beyond the period for which you are applying for funds then you may need to say how you intend to maintain the programme after the grant has been spent.

If you are reapplying for a grant you must demonstrate how the previous grant was used, progress made, problems encountered (if any) and achievements.

Presentation

Presentation matters. As well as being well written, it helps if your application is neatly typed, laid out as clearly as possible, and makes use of photographs, artwork or any other method of making it attractive and readable. If it is handwritten, use *black* ink which will photocopy. Always number pages and put the project name at the top of the page. Check carefully for spelling and typing mistakes and make sure the spelling is consistent.

Other points

It may help to enclose some background material – a leaflet or annual report – with your application, but don't flood the potential funder with enclosures, and always show clearly how the enclosures relate to your application.

Ask someone who is not connected with the project to read it with a critical eye to see if he/she can understand it and that it contains all the necessary information. Remember that the people processing your application may be dealing with hundreds of others, so make yours as easy as possible to understand.

Lobbying

Your work isn't over when you have submitted your application. Find out when it will be considered and contact anyone who may be able to influence the outcome. This may be your local MP or Euro MP, councillors on the Grants Committee, local voluntary sector representatives, etc. Either arrange to meet them or send a letter stating clearly and concisely why your application is important and how and why they should support it.

It is important to distinguish between those who can merely add support to the application, and those who will actually be involved in taking the decision. With central government, the decision-maker is normally ultimately a minister, with whom direct contact is difficult, and best done initially via MPs. With local authorities, the decision will normally be made by a committee which will operate in the open. The key meeting is likely to be open to the public, the date will be known, and it may even be possible to address the meeting. It will certainly be possible – and often a good idea – to meet some members in advance, and perhaps invite them along to see the organisation.

APPENDIX 2

Relations between the Voluntary Sector and Government: A Code for Voluntary Organisations

1 Each voluntary body must regard its freely-chosen aims and objectives as paramount under the law in determining its policy and conduct.
2 Each voluntary body should make a conscious strategic judgement of the maximum proportion of government finance in its total income which is compatible with its basic independence as a voluntary body.
3 Each voluntary body should seek, both in its fund-raising strategy and in its financial dealings with government, to ensure that at least in the medium term it does not allow its dependence on government finance to exceed that prudential proportion.
4 In all financial dealings with government, voluntary bodies should make a distinction between 'arm's-length' support for voluntary activity as such (albeit in a particular sector) and contractual payments on a customer/supplier basis for specific services rendered or functions fulfilled.
5 In the case of 'arm's-length' support voluntary bodies should accept reasonable accountabilty to establish the propriety of the expenditure, but should not accept interferences in policy or measurement of specific effectiveness.
6 In the case of contractual payments for services rendered voluntary bodies should endeavour to ensure that agreements are clearly written to establish what forms of accountability will be expected and should make a judgement at that time, before the contract is signed, as to whether these are practical and reasonable.
7 In costing services to be rendered under contract with government, voluntary bodies should be careful to include realistic provision for overheads, including management time and skills.
8 If, notwithstanding **4** to **7** above, a voluntary body judges in a particular case that its best interests require acceptance of government financial support on terms which lie between the clear poles of 'arm's-length' grants and contractual payments, then they should do so with a full appreciation that this is a compromise and they should make special efforts to ensure that the forms and degrees of accountability expected are precisely defined from the outset.
9 Subject to **1** to **7** above, voluntary bodies should judge all offers of government financial support, whether 'arm's-length' or 'customer/supplier', by reference to that body's aims and objectives and without primary

regard to the possibly different, but overlapping, aims of government policy in offering that funding.

10 Voluntary bodies with charitable status should take care at all times, with appropriate professional advice, to ensure that their activities do not jeopardise their charitable status.

11 Subject to 9 and to the specific aims and objectives of each body, voluntary bodies should assert and exercise their freedom to advocate changes or continuity in public policy, programmes and law to the extent that this is judged to serve the aims and objectives of the body.

12 Voluntary bodies in receipt of public funds should not deliberately become involved, overtly or covertly, in influencing the electoral process at anytime.

13 In dealings with local government, voluntary bodies should bear in mind the principle of comparative advantage, namely that voluntary bodies should mainly do what they typically are good at (including deployment of volunteer effort, speedy and sensitive response to new social and other needs, imaginative and flexible experimentation with new services and techniques of service delivery and real community involvement) and are not in business to take over or inherit those activities which are best provided by statutory bodies (including local authorities' responsibility for strategic social planning and the large-scale expensive permanent personal and social services).

14 Voluntary bodies should bring to NCVO's attention (directly or through their local membership organisations), to reinforce NCVO's existing representation to Whitehall, examples within their experience of lack of co-ordination between Whitehall departments of the impact of new department programmes on the voluntary sector.

15 Any voluntary body which becomes aware of apparent discrimination by government on the grounds of the private political convictions or activities of its leaders or staff should record the facts of the case as precisely as possible at the time, afford an early opportunity for the matter to be discussed by the senior officers or trustees of that body and, if the evidence appears substantial, is invited to report the case to NCVO.

16 Voluntary bodies should consider whether in fact the apparent problems of working in the environment of a government with, as some see it, strong ideological commitments are not fully met by applying the rules above, *and*, if they are not so satisfied, voluntary bodies should seek further discussion with NCVO.

March 1984 (Revised March 1986)

Further information on funding relationships is available in the report of NCVO's Working Party on the Management and Effectiveness of Voluntary Organisations

APPENDIX 3

Powers under which Local Authorities Can Fund Voluntary Organisations

Introduction
A local authority can only spend money on things which it has powers to spend money on – otherwise it is acting illegally and in extreme circumstances its councillors and officers could be surcharged.

This means that when a local authority is approached by a group for a grant, it not only has to decide whether the group's project is a priority and whether it has sufficient resources to give a grant; it also has to be sure that it has the power to give a grant.

In most cases, if local authorities try hard enough, there is nearly always a way of finding the power(s) to fund important projects. Therefore voluntary groups should not accept no for an answer – at least not until all avenues have been fully explored. However, some quite complex situations can arise, in which case groups would be well advised to consult a guide published by NCVO on the subject entitled *Getting in on the Act: A Guide to Local Authorities' Powers to Fund Voluntary Organisations* (see page 79). Some of the main points in this guide are set out below.

The critical questions
There are four main questions which a local authority will need to ask about your voluntary organisation before it can determine whether it has the power to give you a grant:

1 What is your organisation's main *area of concern*?

   Is it education, housing, social services, health, leisure, transport, environment, job creation, training, crime prevention, general advice, support to other local voluntary organisations or some other area of concern?

   The local authority will have a statutory responsibility for some of these areas of concern and if so, will normally be able to fund your organisation under one of the specific Acts relating to them. However, complications arise when the local authority does not have a statutory responsibilty and/or no specific Act relating to your area of concern can be used.

2 Is your organisation concerned exclusively or primarily with the needs of one particular *section of the community*?

   Is it concerned with the needs of black and ethnic minorities, women, disabled people, gay men, lesbians, unemployed people, elderly people, under fives, mentally handicapped people, mentally ill people or some other section of the community?

Provision for some of these groups of people is covered by specific Acts, e.g. the Chronically Sick and Disabled Persons Act or the Child Care Act. But no equivalent legislation exists specially for women, gay men, lesbians or unemployed people, and the position regarding black and ethnic minorities is somewhat uncertain.

3 What kind of *activity* is your organisation involved in?

Does it deliver services, does it provide advice and information, is it involved in redeveloping land, is it involved in campaigning, is it involved in party political activity, is it involved exclusively in charitable activity? Or some combination of these?

Most of the Acts are concerned with service delivery and specific forms of advice and information. Local authorities are expressly prohibited from funding organisations involved in party political activity and their ability to fund campaigning organisations can be limited. (For further details see NCVO's guide *Publish and Still Not Be Damned* listed on page 79.) Some Acts contain specific references to particular activities such as the redevelopment of land or provision of services by charities.

4 What *geographical area* does your organisation cover?

Does it operate in a larger area than the local authority? If so, what proportion of its activities relate to the local authority's area? Which part of the local authority's area does the organisation cover?

A local authority can only fund activity which relates to, or has relevance to, its own area and/or its own residents. However, it can fund activities jointly with other local authorities, and, where appropriate, it can locate certain types of provision outside its own geographical area (e.g. a home for the elderly or an outdoor education centre).

Straightforward cases

In most cases the local authority should have no difficulty in identifying powers to fund a project. These include all the cases

- Where there is *a specific* power to fund or assist voluntary bodies;
- Where to fund a voluntary body would be *incidental* to mainstream functions or powers of a local authority;
- Where assistance is by way of cheap (or free) *goods or services* to appropriate bodies;
- Where the assistance is given through powers to acquire, develop or dispose of *land*.

a **Specific powers** There are a number of specific powers under which the various types of local authority can fund voluntary bodies. One of the best well-known is S. 73 of the Housing Act 1985 under which all district councils and London boroughs can give grants or loans to voluntary bodies concerned with homelessness or matters relating to it, and can provide them with premises, furniture and equipment, and with the services of council staff.

Another, which is fairly widely drawn, is S. 65 of the Health Services and Public Health Act 1968. This enables counties, metropolitan districts and all London boroughs to provide, promote, publicise or give advice about a wide range of social services for children, families, the disabled, the mentally ill and the elderly, and to do so by way of grants, loans, use of premises, or the provision of vehicles, equipment or staff to voluntary organisations.

Others include power to give grants to Dial-a-Ride type schemes under the Transport Act 1985. However, overall, there are relatively few such powers, although any powers which take the form of 'an authority may make, or assist in making, arrangements for . . .' qualify under this heading.

b **Incidental to or calculated to facilitate** A much wider range of possibilities for providing grants and assistance to voluntary organisations is opened up by the use of S. 111 of the Local Government Act 1972. This permits local authorities to do anything which is incidental to or calculated to facilitate the discharge of their functions – which includes the discharge of their powers and duties. So in any situation in which a local authority has a power or a duty, and considers (genuinely and reasonably) that giving a grant to a voluntary organisation would help them to discharge this power, or is incidental to it, they may do so. This combination of S. 111 with mainstream powers is extremely potent. It means that:
- any education authority (a county, metropolitan district, or outer London borough) can fund a wide range of adult education groups, supplementary schools, training projects and school parents associations;
- any social services authority can fund nurseries, day centres, old peoples' groups, associations for disabled people, community care projects, as well as residential homes, community health councils, health visiting schemes, and community help programmes;
- housing authorities can fund housing associations, tenants groups, housing co-operatives, hostels and housing advice centres;
- leisure, libraries and entertainment projects can be funded by all authorities;
- a wide range of environmental improvement projects, conservation schemes, waste recycling projects, wild life projects, local amenity societies and countryside projects can all be funded by most authorities (and many of them by all authorities) by relying on S. 111 in combination with various of the powers described above.

c **Goods and services** Assistance to voluntary organisations in the form of supplying cheap or free goods and services relies on one of those powers which is perfectly adequate to make the practice lawful even though it is doubtful whether this was quite what the politicians had in mind when the relevant Act was passed into law. By the Local Authorities (Goods and Services) Act 1970 local authorities have the power to supply a wide range of goods and services to any 'public body' on *such terms as the parties agree* – and this can include making no charge at all. The 'goods and services' can include equipment, vehicles, maintenance, and administrative, technical or professional services. The definition of 'public body' specifically includes a wide range of national charities and voluntary bodies, but also includes 'community associations'. Advice from leading counsel suggests that this includes law centres, and it will also include most, if not all, local voluntary bodies.

d **Powers in connection with land** Generally, local authority powers to buy and sell land are somewhat restricted, particularly when they are buying land compulsorily. But they do have quite a broad range of powers to buy land by agreement and to do works on it, most notably through S. 120 of the Local Government Act 1972, S. 119 of the Town and Country Planning Act 1971, S. 2 of the Local Authorities Land Act 1963, and S. 89 of the National Parks and Access to the Countryside Act 1949. S. 120 is especially broadly drawn. Local authorities can acquire by agreement any land, whether inside or outside their area, either for any of their functions or for the benefit, improvement, or development of their area. This last phrase is especially important and it is also important that the definition of land appears to include buildings. Nor is it necessary to actually buy the land – the authority only needs to acquire an *interest* in land. So this could include renting offices.

A local authority could therefore obtain premises for the use of many groups whose activities they feel would be to the benefit of their area, but where there are no obvious specific powers to fund the project. Of course, local authorities cannot simply buy a building and give it to such a group, because they are not allowed to dispose of land easily – but they can give the group the use of the premises for up to seven years free of charge, and in these times seven years is about as long a time horizon as any voluntary organisation has.

More complex cases
Although most cases are relatively straightforward, complications can arise. For example, a district council (which does not have social services powers) may be asked to fund a social welfare project. A voluntary organisation may be involved in certain types of campaigning on issues which are not the responsibility of the local authority being asked for a grant. In nearly all cases these complications can be overcome if the local authority is willing to be helpful – often through use of the local authority's research or information-

giving powers (Section 141 and 142 of the Local Government Act 1972). However, readers should consult NCVO's guide on the subject (see below) for further advice.

Finally, there is an important discretionary power available to local authorities under Section 137 of the Local Government Act 1972. Under this power local authorities are empowered to incur expenditure (up to the product of a 2p rate) which 'in their opinion is in the interests of their area or any part of it or all or some of its inhabitants'. The current position regarding S. 137 is explained on pages 67–68.

Richard Gutch
Assistant Director, Local Voluntary Action Department, NCVO

FURTHER READING

Capper, S. *But Is It Legal? Fundraising and the Law*, Bedford Square Press, 1988

Courtney, R. *Planning a Fundraising Strategy*, Northern Ireland Council for Voluntary Action, 1988

Davison, A. *Grants from Europe: How to Get Money and Influence Policy*, 5th edition, Bedford Square Press, 1989

FitzHerbert, L. *A Guide to the Major Grant-Making Trusts*, Directory of Social Change, 1988

Grace, C. and Gutch, R. *Getting in on the Act: A Guide to Local Authorities' Powers to Fund Voluntary Organisations*, NCVO in conjunction with Brent Community Law Centre, 1987

Gutch, R., Miliband, D. and Percival, R. *Publish and Still Not be Damned: A Guide to Section 2 and 2A of the Local Government Act 1986 (as amended by the Local Government Act 1988)*, NCVO, 1989

Norton, M. *A Guide to Company Giving*, Directory of Social Change, 1988

Norton, M. *Major Companies and their Charitable Support*, Directory of Social Change, 1988

Sterrett, P.W. and Sterrett, P.F. *The Complete Guide to Fund Raising*, Mercury Books, 1988

Swainson, A. and Zeff, L. *Please Give Generously! A Guide to Fund Raising*, David and Charles, 1987

Villemur, A. *Directory of Grant-Making Trusts*, Charities Aid Foundation, 1987

NCVO in conjunction with NACRC. *Section 11 – Funding for Black and Ethnic Minorities?*, guidance notes for voluntary groups, NCVO Local Voluntary Action Department, September 1988

For further sources of information see:

Bates, S. *Fund Raising and Grant Aid for Voluntary Organisations: A Guide to the Literature*, Bedford Square Press, 1986

NCVO Information and Intelligence Unit. *Selective Bibliography of Fund-Raising Books and Pamphlets* (NCVO Information Sheet No. 17), NCVO Information and Intelligence Unit, 1988

NCVO Local Development Unit. *Going for Gold: A Guide to a Fundraising Strategy for Local Groups*, NCVO Local Development Unit, 1989

INDEX

adult education, grants for 9–10
ancient monuments 19–20
archaeological excavations, grants for 19
army welfare work 8
artists in residence schemes 32
arts,
    companies 32–3
    funding for 32–3, 43–4
    new projects in 35
    regional associations for 43–4
    training in 32–3

charities, rate relief for 68
children, day care for 22
children's homes 21
coal industry, housing for workers in 60
community care 23–4
community councils, rural, support for 44
community homes 21
Community Industry 54–5
composers, bursaries for 32
conservation areas, grants for 17–18
consumer advice 30
countryside,
    conservation of 36–7, 41–3
    enjoyment of 36–7
    grants for 36
    public access to 36–7
    recreation in 36–7
crafts, support for 37–8
craftsmen,
    business advice for 38
    finance for 38

day care, for under fives 22
derelict land, reclamation of 16
developing countries,
    disaster relief in 29–30
    projects in 27–8
    refugees in 29–30
disabled,
    residential training for 56–7
    sheltered employment for 55
    special help for 56
    training schemes for 55–7
    vocational training for 56
disaster unit 29
drama 32

education, grants for 9–10
educational research, grants for 10
educational services, grants for 10
EEC,
    information on 59
    grants by 58–60
employment training 52–3, 55–7
energy conservation projects 11–12
English Heritage, grant assessment by 18–19
environment, improvement of 12–13
equal opportunities,
    conferences on 39
    research 38–9
equality, racial 34–5
Europe, money from 58–60
European integration, research on 59

films 33
    production of 33
financing, joint 23

goods, users' interests in 30
Government, central
    grants to voluntary organisations by 6–7
    relations with voluntary sector 73–4
grants,
    from central government 6–7
    how to apply for 69–72
    information on 79–80

handicapped,
    employment for 55
    housing for 40
    research into problems of 60
    training for 55–7
health,
    innovative projects 22
    voluntary organisations 20–22, 23
health education research 39
historic buildings,
    advice on 18–19
    repair of 17–18
homelessness, advice on 13–14
hostels,
    bail 26
    probation 26
    for single people 40
housing,
    for elderly 40
    for handicapped 40
    for people with special needs 40
housing associations 1, 40–41
    advice for 40
housing co-operatives, advice for 40
human rights, promotion of 60

immigrants, Commonwealth 26–7
Intermediate Treatment Fund 22

law centres 27
Library, British 34
library collections,
    cataloguing of 34
    conservation of 34
local authorities,
    applying for grants to 62-3, 69-72
    contracts with 62
    funding by 1, 61-3
    grant giving powers of 67-8, 75-9
    grants to voluntary organisations by 61-3
    relations with voluntary sector, 62, 63
    sources of funds for 66-7
    structure of 61-2
    type of grants given by 61-2, 75-9
local government,
    legal framework of 63-8
    structure of 64

marriage guidance councils 25
metroplitan areas, funding arrangements in 64-6
monuments, ancient 19-20

nature conservation 41-3
nature reserves 41-2

offenders,
    hostels for 25
    rehabilitation of 25-6
one-parent families 38
overseas voluntary agencies 20, 28-9

private sector funding 2
public sector funding, changes in 1-3

racial groups,
    equal opportunities for 34-5, 39
    good relations between 34-5
rate relief, changes in 68
road safety 30-1
rural areas,
    economic problems in 44
    social problems in 44
    transport in 45
rural businesses, small 45
rural community councils 44

school leavers, training for 50-1
services, users' interests in 30
sheltered employment 55-7
sport 46-8
sports, encouragement of 46
sports clubs 46-8
sports facilities, provision of 46-8
steel industry, housing for workers in 60

theatre 32
tourist amenities 48
tourist boards 48-50
townscape, preservation of 18
training agencies 52-3
training schemes, vocational 50-1
TV reception, improvement of 45

under-fives, day care of 22
unemployed,
    long-term 52-3
    over 18 years 52-3
    temporary employment for 54
    under 18 years 50-1
urban areas,
    conservation in 17-19
    environmental improvements in 15, 16
    job creation in 15
urban development corporations 16-17
Urban Programme 14-17, 61, 66

village halls 45
vocational training 50-1, 56
voluntary organisations,
    government funding for 6-7, 24-7
    relations with Government 73-4
Voluntary Services Unit 24-5
    advice from 69
voluntary work 21-2
    overseas 28

Women's Institutes, support for 44

young people,
    disadvantaged 54
    vocational training for 50-1
youth exchange visits abroad 57
youth organisations, grants for 9, 10

Other titles in the Practical Guides series:

But Is It Legal? Fundraising and the Law
Employing People in Voluntary Organisations
Getting into Print: An Introduction to Publishing
Helping the Accident Victim: A Guide to Claiming Compensation
Opening the Town Hall Door: An Introduction to Local Government
Organising Your Finances: A Guide to Good Practice
Starting and Running a Voluntary Group
Voluntary Organisations and New Technology
Working Effectively: A Guide to Evaluation Techniques
You Are the Governor: How to be Effective in Your Local School

All books are available through bookshops. In case of difficulty books can be ordered by post direct from Harper & Row Distributors Ltd, Estover Road, Plymouth PL6 7PZ (tel. 0752-705251) adding 12½% to total value of order for post and packing (minimum 30p).